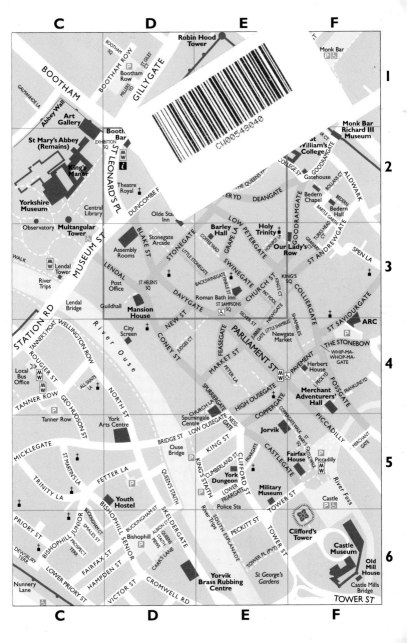

YORK ...MORE THAN A GUIDE

JARROLD

YORK ...MORE THAN A GUIDE

JOHN MCILWAIN

CITY-BREAK GUIDES

Acknowledgements

Photography © Pitkin Publishing by Neil Jinkerson.
Additional photography by kind permission of: Collections; Alan Curtis; Dean & Chapter of York; Peter Gray; VK Guy; Spectrum Colour Library; The Maltings; McArthur Glen Designer Outlet; Middlethorpe Hall; National Centre for Early Music; York Archaeological Trust; York Castle Museum; York City Art Gallery; York Civic Trust; Yorkshire Air Museum.

The publishers wish to thank Kay Hyde (York Tourism Bureau), Gill Cook (Tourist Information Centre), Larch Cardona and Bunny Wright for their invaluable assistance; also the many owners of York businesses for their kindness in allowing us to photograph their premises.

Jarrold is a trading division of Pitkin Publishing.

All information correct at time of going to press but may be subject to change.

Printed in Singapore.
ISBN 978 0 7117 2648 2
2/08

Designer:
Simon Borrough
Editor:
Angela Royston
Artwork and walk maps:
Clive Goodyer
City maps:
The Map Studio Ltd, Romsey, Hants. Main map based on cartography © George Phillip Ltd

Front cover: Statue of Emperor Constantine

Previous page: York Minster

CONTENTS

WELCOME TO YORK

York is without doubt one of Britain's greatest historical cities. Everywhere you go in its compact centre you are surrounded by its history. This began when the Romans set up camp here and then built a fortress and a city they called Eboracum. As successive waves of conquerors invaded, the city was given new names: the Angles called it Eoforwic, the Vikings Jorvik, until the Normans renamed the city York.

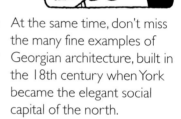

By the Middle Ages, York was the most powerful and prosperous town in northern England. Much of the medieval city can still be seen today, in many buildings, on the streets and all along the ramparts of the city wall, from where you can glimpse the massive medieval Minster rising above the rooftops.

At the same time, don't miss the many fine examples of Georgian architecture, built in the 18th century when York became the elegant social capital of the north.

Add to this a wide variety of quality shops and places to eat, and you will see why York is so popular with visitors. But the great news is that the city has not let world-class quality go to its head. You can expect a genuinely warm welcome in York.

This book aims to give you all the information and suggestions you need to make your stay in York an interesting and enjoyable one.

York Minster

HIGHLIGHTS

There's so much for visitors to see and do in York that a month's stay would hardly do it justice. But a few days are all that most of us have. To help you choose, here are some suggestions on the absolute essentials in this fascinating city.

Outside York Minster

YORK MINSTER
map E2

The Minster is top of the list for most people who come to York. For nearly 1,000 years this great cathedral, the biggest of its kind in Northern Europe, has cast its aura over the city. It began as a Saxon church built on the site where Constantine was proclaimed Roman emperor. A Norman building replaced it, to be succeeded by the splendid medieval cathedral we see today. You can explore its rich history through the superb new audio tour of the foundations and treasury. The real splendour, however, is up above. Amongst many marvels, the Minster houses Britain's most ancient and beautiful stained glass, including the largest such window in Britain. The view of York from the top of the tower on a clear day is alone worth a visit to the Minster.

Look for the east window behind the altar, the choir screen which depicts the kings of England from William the Conqueror to Henry VI, the Lantern Tower, the rose window in the south transept, and the dragon's head high above the nave.

Open: daily for services 7.00; for visitors: Mon–Sat 9.00–16.45, Sun 12.30–15.45. Opening times subject to services. Please ring to check
Entry: over £5
Further information: pages 52–55

FIRE IN THE MINSTER
A bolt of lightning struck the Minster in 1984, the ensuing blaze doing severe damage to the south transept. But the worst event of modern times was in 1829, when religious fanatic Mad Martin set fire to the choirstalls.

York Minster and the Bar Walls

A WALK THROUGH YORK'S MEDIEVAL STREETS

In the shadow of the Minster huddle Britain's finest surviving medieval streets, where timber-framed houses lean improbably towards each other across narrow lanes and alleys, known locally as 'snickelways'. Stonegate (map D3) was built to serve the Roman garrison and has been in daily use for almost 2,000 years. Along here Emperor Constantine processed in triumph and his legionaries marched. Goodramgate (map F2) gets its name from Gutherun, a Viking chief-tain; Petergate from the patron saint of the Minster. In these tiny thoroughfares lived the craftsmen who worked on the great cathedral. Although most of the cottages are now attractive shops, you have only to look upwards to turn the clock back to the Middle Ages.

For an even more vivid experience, Barley Hall (map E3), just off Stonegate, is a beautifully restored medieval house. A new audio tour gives a real taste of life 700 years ago and is narrated by one of York's best-known former residents – Dame Judi Dench. A short walk away is the narrowest and most famous medieval street of all, the Shambles (map F4), once a lane of butchers' establish-ments but now home to a variety of fascinating shops. A recent addition is Past Images, a specialist photographic studio offering visitors the chance to have a high-quality portrait taken in authentic period costume: Viking, medieval or Victorian – choose your era!

Further information: pages 33, 44 and 48

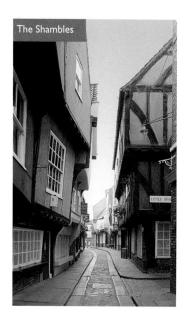

The Shambles

JORVIK
Coppergate Walk; map E5

No visit to York would be complete without a visit to Jorvik, the Viking city. For a century, Ivor the Boneless, Eric Bloodaxe and their Viking pals made their capital here. In the 1970s archaeol-ogists unearthed a Viking settlement in Coppergate and now this has been recreated on the actual location. For 20 hi-tech minutes you can journey in a time car to experience the sights, sounds and smells of life in AD 975.

Open: check www.jorvik-viking-centre.co.uk for opening times

Entry: under £10, joint ticket with DIG (page 30) available

Further information: page 38

National Railway Museum

NATIONAL RAILWAY MUSEUM
Leeman Road

Voted best European Museum 2001, the NRM is a sparkling display of everything to do with railways over two centuries of history. The centrepiece is the Great Hall, where massive locomotives, steam and diesel, stand around a working turntable. See how it all began with ancient black puffers, and then move on to the heyday of steam and the superb, streamlined *Mallard*. Don't miss Queen Victoria's royal saloon. Finally, the impressive Japanese Bullet Train brings you back to the present. There are also many interactive displays, video shows and working demonstrations.

Open: daily; 10.00–18.00. Closed 24–26 Dec only
Entry: free
Further information: page 42

CASTLE MUSEUM
Eye of York; map F6

The finest and most popular museum of social history in Britain. Don't let the word 'museum' put you off. What you have here are stunning recreations of ordinary people's lives from the past. The museum owes its beginnings to John Kirk, a country doctor based in nearby Pickering, who was distressed to see the everyday reminders of Victorian life being consigned to rubbish tips or simply left to rot. He resolved to buy up or rescue what he could for posterity. Now what was once the County Gaol is home to his collection and the thousands of things which have been added since the museum opened in 1938. Wander through Victorian and Edwardian streets; go into the shops and houses; peer into furnished rooms of long ago. There are costumes from bygone ages as well, and everyday things from 20th-century childhood – the toys our grandparents played with, the clothes they wore, and even the loos they sat on!

Open: daily 09.30–17.00
Entry: under £10
Further information: page 34

A WALK ALONG THE BAR WALLS

In this city of delights, one of York's prime features is its splendid city wall. The Romans had the idea first, but what we see today was built in the 13th and 14th centuries. A double plus for visitors are the walkways which run for miles along the battlements, affording superb views over the city. A stroll along the top is a great way to get your bearings. And

Castle Museum

Bar Walls

it need not wear you out, because you can get up and down at several places around the city.

As you walk, look out for the bars – no, not the plentiful York pubs, but the four stunning medieval gateways called bars that punctuate the walls. Bootham Bar is by far the most ancient gate to the city; Walmgate Bar retains its original outer defensive barbican; Micklegate, the ancient entrance of kings, houses a small museum charting the city's history; and Monk Bar, with its working portcullis, hides a quirky museum devoted to Richard III. If you don't want to do the entire circuit, the best stretch of the wall to sample is probably the one which offers the best views of the Minster, from Bootham Bar to Monk Bar (see pages 28–29).

Open: daily 8.00–dusk
Entry: free
Further information: pages 32, 33, 40 and 50

MUSEUM GARDENS
map B2/3–C2/3

This green haven near the city centre is more than just a quiet place to stroll or to sit and feed the ducks. Within the gardens are the Multangular Tower, the only remaining part of the original Roman wall (see page 41), the elegant ruins of St Mary's Abbey (see page 47), the Hospitium – the guesthouse for the abbey (see page 37) – and the excellent Yorkshire Museum (see page 55).
Open: daily; summer 8.00–20.00; winter 8.00–17.30
Entry: free
Further information: page 41

GATES AND BARS
Over 40 of York's thoroughfares have the suffix 'gate', from the Viking 'gata' meaning street. The city's medieval entrances at Bootham, Monk, Micklegate and Walmgate were therefore known as bars to avoid confusion.

Walmgate Bar

Betty's Tearooms

AFTERNOON TEA AT BETTY'S
St Helen's Square; map D3

In a city of superb teashops, this is *the* tearooms to go to. Presiding over St Helen's Square in glassy, art deco splendour (inspired by the liner *Queen Mary*), Betty's has traditionally-attired waitresses serving delicious snacks, lunches and famous afternoon teas.

Further information: page 72

GHOST WALKS

York is officially the most haunted city in Europe, which accounts for the number of spooky guided walks on offer after the sun goes down. You will laugh, you will scream, but you will never forget. Most walks start at 19.30 or 20.00 from several points liberally advertised around the city.

Further information: page 80

AND FINALLY ...

York has too many highlights to include here, but the snickelways (see page 29), Merchant Adventurers' Hall (see page 39), the view from Clifford's Tower (see page 35), Treasurer's House (see page 49), Fairfax House (see page 35), boat trips on the Ouse (see page 83), and the DIG (see page 30), a natural, hands-on follow up to Jorvik, are all a quintessential part of a visit to York.

> **ALL SNICKELWAYS LEAD TO . . .**
> St Sampson's Square is the focal point of York's snickelways, because for centuries it was known as Thursday Market, where local people came from far and wide to buy and sell produce.

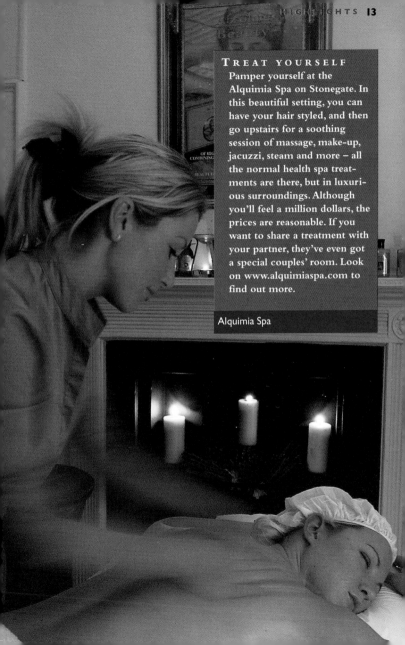

TREAT YOURSELF

Pamper yourself at the Alquimia Spa on Stonegate. In this beautiful setting, you can have your hair styled, and then go upstairs for a soothing session of massage, make-up, jacuzzi, steam and more – all the normal health spa treatments are there, but in luxurious surroundings. Although you'll feel a million dollars, the prices are reasonable. If you want to share a treatment with your partner, they've even got a special couples' room. Look on www.alquimiaspa.com to find out more.

Alquimia Spa

YORK'S HERITAGE

What makes York so special is the fact that its long, rich history is still here in the city for us to explore and enjoy today.

Mansion House

York's first fortress, that of the Roman Ninth Legion, was founded in AD 71. Constantine was crowned emperor here in 306 and massive, multi-sided towers were added to the walls. One of them still stands in Museum Gardens (see page 41), and remains of the garrison can be seen in the Minster's undercroft (see page 53). The Romans' main street, the Via Praetoria, survives as today's Stonegate, while a Roman bath lives on in the unlikely setting of a pub cellar (see page 78).

The Minster was founded in the 7th century when York was the chief town of the Angles' province, Northumbria. The Viking raiders in the 9th century brought many years of uneasy, bloody rule. Jorvik was their capital, and in

Barley Hall

FITTING REMINDER

At Past Images, in York's historic Shambles, you can have your photographic portrait taken in costume which matches your surroundings. A choice of outfits will transform you into a Viking, a medieval burgher or a Victorian – it's up to you.

York Railway Station

today's Jorvik (see page 38) we can see how they lived in the actual place where they lived. The rule of Wessex followed, to be eclipsed by the Norman invasion: Clifford's Tower (see page 35) is built on the mound of the original Norman keep.

Without doubt York's richest heritage is medieval. The Minster (completed in 1472) dominates narrow lanes which once housed the people who built it. Tucked within them is the restored Barley Hall (see page 33) in Coffee Yard which gives a true feel of life in the Middle Ages. The Merchant Adventurers' Hall in Piccadilly (see page 39) adds another, wealthier dimension.

King's Manor (see page 39), although medieval in origin, is Tudor in appearance, while the ancient pews of Holy Trinity Church (see page 36) represent the Jacobean era of James I. A visit to the beautifully restored Fairfax House (see page 35) is the best way to sample the

Georgian way of life and style of architecture. The Mansion House (map ref D3) and the Assembly Rooms (see page 30) are splendid examples, too.

York's railway station is a nationally famous demonstration of the Victorian ability to combine industrial ingenuity with creative design, while the 1990s' CGU building near Lendal Bridge (map C3) represents York's later additions to its fine architectural heritage.

Fairfax House

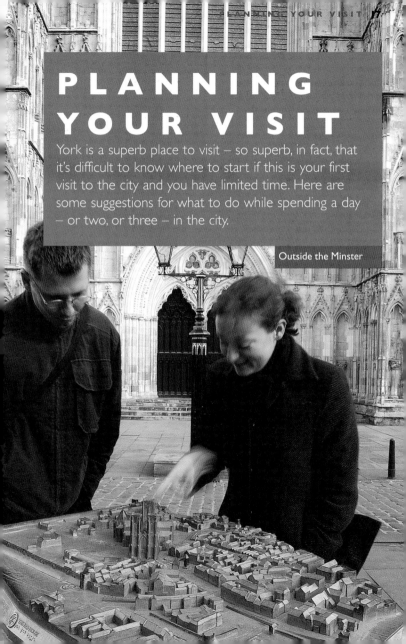

PLANNING YOUR VISIT

York is a superb place to visit – so superb, in fact, that it's difficult to know where to start if this is your first visit to the city and you have limited time. Here are some suggestions for what to do while spending a day – or two, or three – in the city.

Outside the Minster

WHAT TO DO IN ONE DAY

You can get an instant feel for the city by riding on an open-top bus. Tours start and stop at various places and last about an hour (see page 83 for details).

York's crowning glory is its medieval Minster (see pages 52–55) and no visit would be complete without seeing it properly. Guided tours take around 45 minutes. From the Minster's south door, it's only a few paces through Minster Gates (a street – no gates!) to Stonegate (see pages 48–49), an ancient and delightful shopping street. Stonegate also includes cafés, some lovely medieval tearooms, and ancient pubs which serve hot drinks, and something stronger.

Now you have a choice. You may choose the National Railway Museum (see page 42); the quickest and easiest way to get there is by road train which leaves (Apr–Oct) near the Minster's west end. You should allow up to two hours for your visit, and you can also have lunch there if you wish. Come back for Jorvik (see page 38). Pre-book Jorvik to avoid queuing for an hour or two.

Or, if trains don't excite you, go back up Stonegate towards the Minster, turn right into High Petergate and follow it down

National Railway Museum

to King's Square. Just beyond you'll find the Shambles (see page 48), York's most famous medieval street. Off it to the right is the colourful Newgate Market (see page 43) and further right is Parliament Street (see page 44), where there's always street entertainment or something else interesting going on. At the bottom of Parliament Street, cross Coppergate into Coppergate Walk for Jorvik (see above).

Turn right below Jorvik for the Georgian splendour of Fairfax House (see page 35) on Castlegate. Then head back up the hill in the direction of the Minster (via the Shambles if you didn't visit them earlier). Once you've found St Helen's Square at the top of Davygate and Coney Street, treat yourself by dropping into Betty's (see pages 72–73) for a traditional afternoon tea.

York Minster

Boat trips on the River Ouse

Castle Museum

WHAT TO DO IN TWO DAYS

One day in York is good – two days is better! The suggestions for one day should also be part of your two-day itinerary. Do the bus tour (see page 83) and be certain to see the Minster – but why not take a bit longer than those who have only one day? If you're fit, climb up the tower for the view or go down into the Undercroft (or both!) – allow two hours if you do. Stroll along Stonegate, amble the Shambles and don't forget to visit Jorvik – having pre-booked, of course.

For a two-day stay, a visit to the Castle Museum (see page 34), the most popular folk museum in Britain, is a must. It paints a unique and unforgettable picture of how people have lived in England over the centuries. Allow over an hour for this. From the museum it's just a few strides (plus a short, steep climb of steps) to enjoy the view of the city from the top of Clifford's Tower (see page 35).

HANSOM CAB

Joseph Hansom (1803–82) was christened at Bar Convent and became a Micklegate architect, but is famous for inventing the hansom cab, a kind of taxi which plied its trade in every Victorian city in Britain.

Five minutes' walk away, on the other side of Tower Street, is King's Staith on the River Ouse. You can take a leisurely one-hour boat cruise from here (see page 83). If the weather is bad, an alternative is the York Dungeon (see page 51) on Clifford Street, telling York's story the gory way – but it's only for those of a strong constitution!

Little Betty's

For lunch, Russell's of Coppergate (see page 75) supplies traditional English roasts served from the carvery (see the upstairs room if you can). Pub-lunch options include the Three Tuns in Coppergate or the Golden Fleece in Pavement. Or you could earn your pub lunch by walking for 10 minutes or so to the Royal Oak (see page 78), not far from the end of Goodramgate (through the Shambles, King's Square and then right). From here you can walk along the Bar Walls from Monk Bar to Bootham Bar (see page 28).

If you feel like afternoon tea, you can choose from the atmospheric St William's College (see page 75) near the Minster, Beams on Stonegate or, close by, Little Betty's (smaller, but just as good as its namesake).

St William's College

WHAT TO DO IN THREE DAYS

If you're lucky enough to have three days in this interesting city, another whole raft of options opens up for you. The suggestions for one and two days cover the most popular sights, but some of the other sections in this book will be useful in planning a longer visit. If you enjoy a stroll, take a look at the walks mentioned on pages 24–29. If you're a shopaholic, your extra day gives you more time to explore York's many shops. Check out pages 58–70.

Further historical places to visit within the city include the Treasurer's House (see page 49) behind the Minster, with its rooms beautifully decorated and furnished in different period styles, and the quirky Richard III Museum (see page 46) at Monk Bar, but keep away if

Red House antiques (page 67)

KING'S SQUARE

The open space that is King's Square is not as ancient as it looks. Once the site of the south-east gateway to the Roman fortress, it was created in 1937 by the demolition of medieval Christ Church.

City Screen (page 57)

How to Save Yourself Money

For a single outlay, the York Pass gives you free entry to all the city's museums and attractions; also to some bus tours and boat trips. A one-day card is around £20, two-day around £30, and three-day around £35.

You can buy the York Pass from the city's two Tourist Information Centres, or you can order ahead via the Internet: www.YorkPass.com

you lack a sense of humour! Barley Hall (see page 33), off Stonegate, is a genuine medieval house rescued from oblivion and restored as it was. The Yorkshire Museum (see page 55) in its charming gardens contains many real artefacts from the county's history, including the exquisite Middleham Jewel and the Anglo-Saxon York Helmet.

Artefacts from the Yorkshire Museum

Possible tours and trips within the city are suggested on pages 82–83. Alternatively, you may like to see the beautiful countryside around York. You'll find some ideas for easy day tours on pages 88–90.

Stonegate (page 48)

WALKS

York is so full of hidden treasures, that the best way to get the most out of the city is on foot. Below are three walks, one for those who like history, one for shoppers, and one which includes a bit of everything.

SIGHTSEEING WALK

This takes in a rich variety of historical sights, all of them worth exploring further. Allow up to two hours, or more if you intend to visit places on the way.

Start at the gates to Museum Gardens (see page 41) just above Lendal Bridge. Enter the gardens and keep the ancient wall to your right, passing the Roman Multangular Tower (see page 41) alongside King's Manor. By the Art Gallery (see page 51), cross the road and go through Bootham Bar (see page 33) to High Petergate.

In just 30 metres (40 yards), turn left into a snickelway by the Hole in the Wall pub. Go through Precentor's Court to the Minster (see pages 52–55). Follow the path left of the Minster through Dean's Court. Turn right into Minster Yard, past the Treasurer's House (see page 49) and St William's College (see page 47), where you might like to stop for coffee. Hug the end of the Minster and go round to your right.

RED DEVIL
The little red devil which sits outside No. 33 Stonegate is not to show that the inhabitants were satanic in any way, but rather to mark what was once a printer's shop. Printers' devils were the boys who had to carry hot metal type.

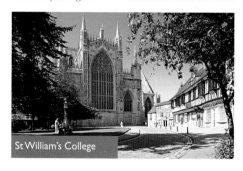

St William's College

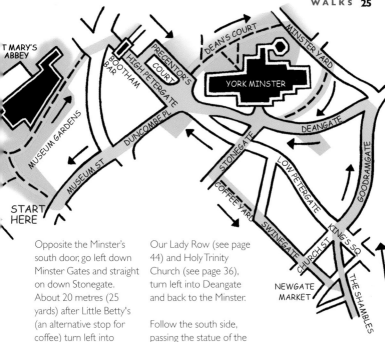

Opposite the Minster's south door, go left down Minster Gates and straight on down Stonegate. About 20 metres (25 yards) after Little Betty's (an alternative stop for coffee) turn left into Coffee Yard. Pass Barley Hall (see page 33) into Swinegate – you are now in bistro territory!

Straight across Church Street, head for the stalls of Newgate Market (see page 43). Leave the market at one of three exits to the Shambles (see page 48). Explore the street, then head up to King's Square (open-air food and drink here). By Boots turn right into Goodramgate. After

Our Lady Row (see page 44) and Holy Trinity Church (see page 36), turn left into Deangate and back to the Minster.

Follow the south side, passing the statue of the Roman emperor Constantine, to the west end. Cross by the Dean Court Hotel to

Duncombe Place. Follow that to Museum Street, and so back to your starting place.

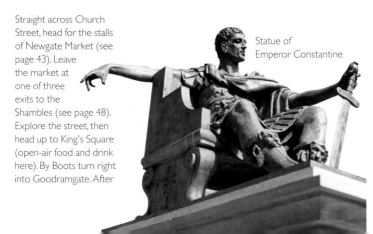

Statue of Emperor Constantine

SHOPPERS' WALK

This walk includes a cornucopia of small, independently run shops and too many coffee shops and eating places to mention! Allow a morning.

Gem Rock, Stonegate

Starting at the statue of Emperor Constantine at York Minster's south door, cross to Minster Gates. Continue straight on down the right-hand side of Stonegate. Here you will find gifts, jewellery and clothes, as well as fine china. At St Helen's Square, where you will find Betty's Tearooms (see pages 72–73), turn round and retrace your steps but turn right at the teddy bear shop into Little Stonegate, where there is Laura Ashley and the Rubicon veggie restaurant.

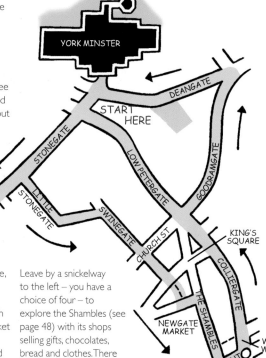

Turn right into Swinegate, where there are plenty of bistros and designer shops; cross over Church Street to Newgate Market (see page 43). Here is a deli, books, clothes – and much more.

Leave by a snickelway to the left – you have a choice of four – to explore the Shambles (see page 48) with its shops selling gifts, chocolates, bread and clothes. There are plenty of tearooms

Crabtree & Evelyn, Stonegate

here too. Go down to Pavement, left and left again into Whip-Ma-Whop-Ma-Gate and then into Colliergate. Here you will find shops selling jewellery, clothes and homeware, as well as a post office.

Continue through King's Square, stopping perhaps at its food stalls, and straight ahead to Low Petergate for clothes, art, and jewellery. Turn by Boots into Goodramgate, which has all sorts of interesting, independent shops further down. Turn left into Deangate back to the Minster where the walk began.

Newgate Market

W H I P - M A - W H O P - M A - G A T E
The quaint name of Whip-Ma-Whop-Ma-Gate, the tiny street off Pavement, has provoked much discussion. Was it a place where people were flogged? The best explanation is that it derives from 'whit-nour-whot-nour', a medieval expression of scorn, roughly translated as 'call this a street?'

A BIT OF EVERY-THING WALK

This walk includes a range of historic places, a walk on the city wall and some delightful shops that you will see on the way. Allow up to two hours, but more if you intend to visit places en route.

Start at the Castle Museum's front door (see page 34). Clifford's Tower (see page 35) faces you. Cross the car park heading towards the tiny River Foss on the right. A path behind Fenwicks' store hugs the riverside. Emerge on Piccadilly. Cross the road to the Merchant Adventurers' Hall (see page 39). Go down the steps, round the hall, through a passage and left into Fossgate.

At the top of Fossgate, go briefly left then right into the Shambles (see page 48). Follow this tiny street to King's Square. At Boots go down Goodramgate and follow it to Monk Bar (see page 40). Go up the narrow steps to the Bar Walls (see page 32) and the Richard III Museum (see page 46). Turn left along the wall to Bootham

FROM PRIESTS TO POVERTY
The area known as the Bedern, off Goodramgate, has had a chequered history. In medieval times it housed the Vicars Choral, priests employed at the Minster to say masses for the wealthy dead. By Queen Victoria's reign, the area was a slum.

Bar. Note that the Bar Walls can be slippery in wet weather, so you may prefer to go directly to Bootham Bar via the south side of the Minster.

At Bootham Bar, cross the road, bearing left to King's Manor. Go down the side of the Manor into Museum Gardens (see page 41). There are options here to look at the Yorkshire Museum (see page 55), St Mary's Abbey ruins (see page 47) and the Hospitium (see page 37). Passing the Multangular Tower (see page 41), keep left for the gates out of the gardens. Cross the road to Lendal. Keep straight on to St Helen's Square (see page 46). Here you can take in the Mansion House and Betty's (see page 72) before continuing down Coney Street, Spurriergate, Nessgate and Castlegate. You may just have time for Fairfax House (see page 35) before returning to your starting point.

The Hospitium

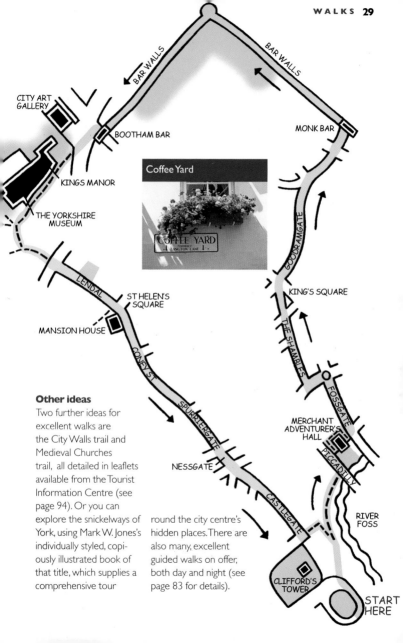

BAR WALLS

BAR WALLS

CITY ART
GALLERY

BOOTHAM BAR

MONK BAR

KINGS MANOR

THE YORKSHIRE
MUSEUM

Coffee Yard

COFFEE YARD
LANGTON LANE

GOODRAMGATE

KING'S SQUARE

LENDAL

ST HELEN'S
SQUARE

THE SHAMBLES

MANSION HOUSE

CONEY ST

FOSSGATE

MERCHANT
ADVENTURER'S
HALL

SPURRIERGATE

PICCADILLY

Other ideas

Two further ideas for
excellent walks are
the City Walls trail and
Medieval Churches
trail, all detailed in leaflets
available from the Tourist
Information Centre (see
page 94). Or you can
explore the snickelways of
York, using Mark W. Jones's
individually styled, copi-
ously illustrated book of
that title, which supplies a
comprehensive tour

NESSGATE

CASTLEGATE

round the city centre's
hidden places. There are
also many, excellent
guided walks on offer,
both day and night (see
page 83 for details).

RIVER
FOSS

CLIFFORD'S
TOWER

START
HERE

SIGHTSEEING

Ancient Chinese saying: 'In the greatest happiness is the greatest sadness.' For visitors to York, the happy thing is that there is so much to see and do. The sad thing is that for most people, there isn't the time to fit it all in! This section covers the main sights to see.

In terms of opening hours, summer begins on the last weekend in March and lasts until the end of October (when clocks revert to Greenwich Mean Time). Also if you're thinking of coming to York in winter, remember that most places are closed on Christmas Day, Boxing Day and New Year's Day.

DIG
St Saviourgate; map F4

DIG

Ever fancied being an archaeologist? DIG gives visitors a unique and exciting chance to get hands-on experience of real objects which the Romans and Vikings left behind: shoes, pottery, combs – even ice-skates! With plenty of support from the staff, you will learn how to make sense of the things you find, and gain a lasting insight into what life was like in York 1,000 years or more ago. The wheelchair-friendly Sensory Garden includes hearing posts and braille text. Many school parties come here, but independent visitors are made very welcome.

Open: Mon–Fri 10.00–17.00
Entry: over £5, joint ticket with Jorvik available
Tel: 01904 654324
Website:
www.jorvik-viking-centre.co.uk/dig
Disabled access: full

Assembly Rooms
Blake Street; map D3
It's appropriate that these magnificent Italianate rooms, built by Lord Burlington between 1730 and 1735 in the style of Palladio, should now be an elegant Italian restaurant called ASK (see page 77) that seats 200 people. Passers-by can easily peek in through the entrance, but if you have a meal you can enjoy the full Georgian splendour. In case you are wondering, assemblies were winter entertainments of the 17th and 18th centuries, mainly card games and dancing – very Jane Austen.

Restaurant in the Assembly Rooms

Open: daily, 12.00–23.00. Closed
25 Dec
Tel: 01904 637254
Disabled access: full

Bar Convent Museum
Blossom Street; map B6
This 1787 building, near the station,
fulfils four functions: a Roman Catholic
convent, a budget-priced café, a do-it-
yourself bed-and-breakfast place, and a
museum. The museum focuses on reli-
gion in pre-Reformation England and
also covers the history of Christianity in
the north of England. Look for the splendid chapel and the tiled courtyard.
Open: Mar–Dec: Mon–Fri 10.00–17.00
(last admission 16.00). Closed Good
Fri–Easter Mon, 20 Dec–1 Feb
Entry: under £5
Tel: 01904 643238
Website: www.bar-convent.org.uk
Disabled access: full
Other facilities: café (see page 72),
bed and breakfast (see page 93), and
gift shop

Bar Walls
Marked in red on the map
York's unique walls, known as the Bar
Walls, stretch for nearly 5 kilometres
(3 miles) around the city. The Romans
built the original version to defend their
garrison, but their efforts were pulled
down and expanded by successive
invaders. The magnificent wall we see
today was built in the 13th and 14th
centuries from limestone quarried locally
and brought into the city by river. In
some places it stands atop Roman foundations, and also contains Anglo-Saxon

work. The walls are punctuated by four
magnificent gateways, known as bars –
see Bootham Bar (page 33), Micklegate
Bar (page 40), Monk Bar (page 40), and
Walmgate Bar (page 50) for details.

The views from the wall over the city
are marvellous, and a stroll along the
elevated walkway is an essential part
of any visit. You can access it at several
places, the most used section being
that which links the railway station with
Lendal Bridge. The finest section to walk
is between Bootham Bar and Monk Bar
(see page 28), offering lovely views of
the Minster from a new angle. The highest section – not for those who dislike
heights – is from Micklegate Bar to
Lendal. A word of warning: in wet
weather and with autumn leaves, the
steps and walls become slippery, so
make sure you wear the right shoes and
watch your footing.
Open: daily 8.00–dusk
Entry: free
Disabled access: none

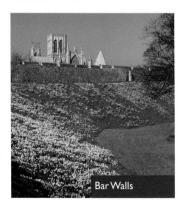
Bar Walls

SCOTS WHA' HAE!
According to an ancient law, it is apparently still legal to shoot a Scotsman with a bow and arrow, but only if you spot him within the city walls and after dark.

Barley Hall
Coffee Yard; map E3

William Snawsell was one of the richest and most important men in York, a city goldsmith and Lord Mayor. In 1483, he was living with his family in Barley Hall. The hall is a restored medieval town house, whose beauty had lain hidden for centuries under ugly additions. Now, superb audio tours help you eavesdrop on the Alderman's busy days and get a real feel for life in York in medieval times. Costumed events take place at weekends in summer.

Open: Tue–Sun 10.00–16.00 plus Bank Holiday Mondays
Entry: under £5
Tel: 01904 610275
Website:
www.barleyhall.org.uk
Disabled access: limited
Other facilities: gift shop

Bootham Bar
map D2

The oldest of York's fine gateways stands a stone's throw from the west end of the Minster. Its central arch bears the rounded shape that is characteristic of Norman architecture. In the centuries which followed its building, guards would wait here to accompany travellers through the dangerous Forest of Galtres, which lay to the north of the city. A narrow stairway here gives access to the Bar Walls. The painting below of Bootham Bar hangs in York City Art Gallery (see page 51).

Bootham Bar

BIG PETER
Big Peter, the Minster bell which chimes at noon, weighs over ten tonnes. It is the third heaviest bell in England and is thought to have the deepest tone in Europe. Its chimes can be heard all over the city centre.

Castle Museum
Eye of York; map F6

Many visitors leave York's award-winning Castle Museum in a state of dreamy euphoria. This is the most popular folk museum in Britain, and it is not hard to see why. The theme throughout may be everyday objects of everyday life, but don't get the impression there is anything humdrum about the place.

It was started by Dr Kirk, a country GP who, from the 1890s, rescued household items destined for oblivion. In 1938 his huge collection found a home in the former Debtors' Prison (Dick Turpin spent the three months before his execution here, and you can visit his cell). Things have developed rapidly since then. For one thing, the museum boasts one of the largest collections of historic costumes in the country. Fascinating displays recapture the lives of departed generations – not to mention our own and parents' childhoods.

The re-created rooms of yesteryear are wonderful, but the jewels in the museum's crown are the life-size Victorian and Edwardian cobbled streets, where you can wander in and out of shops and cottages, parlours and prisons.

DON'T MISS

The Victorian street.
The Edwardian street with the gypsy caravan.
From Cradle to Grave: the trappings of birth, marriage and death.
Open: daily 9.30–17.00
Entry: under £10
Tel: 01904 687687
Website: www.york.castle.museum
Disabled access: limited

Castle Museum

Clifford's Tower
map F6

When William the Conqueror's men made this mound for the keep to their castle they knew what they were doing, for the view over the city is magnificent. The wooden tower they put on top was destroyed in one of the blackest episodes of York's history: the massacre in 1190 of 150 Jews who sought sanctuary here during anti-Semitic riots. Henry III's men rebuilt the tower in stone, but it was damaged in the 18th century, and today is largely an empty shell. The view still draws many visitors who are willing to do a bit of climbing. Helpful displays describe in detail what you can see. A further display in the gatehouse tells the story of castles through the ages.

Open: daily; Apr–Sep: 10.00–18.00; Oct: 10.00–17.00; Nov–Mar: 10.00–16.00
Entry: under £5
Tel: 01904 646940
Website: www.cliffordstower.com or www.visityork.org
Disabled access: limited

Fairfax House

Fairfax House
Castlegate; map F5

One of the best historic-house museums in England, Fairfax House is the finest example of a Georgian town house in York, and perhaps in Britain. It has had a chequered history – its grand upper rooms were once used as a dance hall, and it was rescued from near collapse in 1984. Fully restored to its original glory, complete with magnificent carvings and plaster ceilings, it now houses the Noel Terry collection of 18th-century furniture and clocks.

Open: Mon–Thu and Sat 11.00–17.00, Sun 13.30–17.00, Fri guided tours only at 11.00, 14.00
Entry: under £10
Tel: 01904 655543
Website: www.fairfaxhouse.co.uk
Disabled access: none
Other facilities: gift shop

Clifford's Tower

Guildhall

Guildhall
Access from St Helen's Square; map D3
York's 15th-century Guildhall on the
bank of the River Ouse is where the city
fathers have met since medieval times.
The building suffered badly during the air
raids of 1942, but has been wonderfully
restored. Particularly worth seeing are
the Council Chamber, an exact recon-
struction of the original, and a stained-
glass panel depicting the city's history.

Open: May–Oct: Mon–Fri 9.00–17.00,
Sat 10.00–17.00, Sun 14.00–17.00;
Nov–April: daily 9.00–17.00
Entry: free
Tel: 01904 613161
Disabled access: limited

Herbert House
Pavement; map F4
Pavement was one of York's earliest
paved streets, first mentioned in 1329.
Herbert House, now a shoe shop, is a
fine timber-framed building, which was
home to Sir Thomas Herbert, a close
friend of Charles I – so close that he sat
with Charles on the night before the
monarch's execution in 1649. Pavement,
too, was the scene of many public
executions in the past.

Holy Trinity Church
Hornpot Lane; map E3
Holy Trinity Church is mentioned in the

Holy Trinity Church

famous Domesday Book commissioned by William the Conqueror in about 1086. Besides its ancient and lovely stained glass, its most unusual feature is the box pews which date from the reign of James I and which were rented out to rich families. In most English churches and cathedrals, the Victorians unceremoniously ripped these out, but at Holy Trinity they survive in sombre splendour. Access to the church can also be gained from Goodramgate.

DON'T MISS

The squint – a slit cut in the wall of the nave so that priests could see to celebrate mass simultaneously at the high altar and in the side chapel.
Open: summer Mon–Sat 10.00–17.00, Sun 12.00–17.00; winter Tue–Sat 10.00–16.00 (subject to daylight)
Tel: 01904 613451
Disabled access: limited

The Hospitium
Museum Gardens; map B3
In the Middle Ages, guests of St Mary's Abbey would stay in the hospitium, a stone house in the abbey grounds. The abbey is now an elegant ruin and in its grounds is a botanical garden, but the hospitium remains, a delightful sample of the medieval builder's art. It is not open to the public, but at weekends a craft fair is held on the ground floor.

The Hospitium
CRAFT FAIR

Jorvik
Coppergate Walk; map E5

York owes its name to the Vikings, who built their biggest city, Jorvik, by the River Ouse 1,100 years ago. In the late 1970s archaeologists uncovered the beautifully preserved remains of an ancient Viking street – today's Coppergate. Now on that site, 21st-century technology has recreated ancient Jorvik exactly as it was one day in AD 975. Aboard your time car you can journey back through the centuries to witness the sights, sounds (and smells!) of everyday Viking life in Coppergate – an unforgettable experience. Pre-booking is strongly recommended in high season, when you can queue for anything up to two hours, although it's likely you'll be entertained as you queue!

Open: check website
Entry: under £10, joint ticket with DIG (page 30) available
Tel: 01904 543400
Website: www.jorvik-viking-centre.co.uk
Disabled: full, but essential to pre-book
Other facilities: café and gift shop

DICK TURPIN

Dick Turpin was not the chivalrous highwayman that legend made him out to be. Rather, he was a merciless cut-throat who was quite happy to roast a woman in front of a fire to extract the whereabouts of her jewellery.

Jorvik

Merchant Adventurers' Hall

King's Manor

King's Manor
Exhibition Square; map C2

This fine house, dating from the
13th century, was home to the Abbot
of St Mary's. Apart from the Sheriff
of Nottingham, the Abbot was Robin
Hood's number one enemy, and features
in all the films! When St Mary's was
closed by Henry VIII it became in turn a
royal palace, the residence of the military
governors and a school. It is now part of
York University. Tourists can walk around
the grounds and see the outside of the
building. The inner courtyards are particularly worth a look.
Entry: free
Information line: 01904 432030
Website: www.york.ac.uk
Disabled access: limited

Mansion House
see St Helen's Square

Merchant Adventurers' Hall
Fossgate; map F4

In medieval times, England's great cities
were ruled by guilds of merchants and
craftsmen. York, then an international
port, was no exception. The most
powerful guild was the Merchant
Adventurers, who controlled the city's
(and England's) cloth trade. Their
hall with its hospital and chapel, built
1357–61, is one of the finest in Europe.
Particularly impressive is the huge
upstairs room with its marvellous oak
floor, which over the centuries has
acquired a roller-coaster look, caused
by moving foundations.
Open: Apr–Sep: Mon–Thu 9.00–17.00,
Fri–Sat 9.00–15.30, Sun 12.00–16.00;
Oct–June: Mon–Sat 9.00–15.30.
Closed 23 Dec–2 Jan, Sundays Oct–Mar
Entry: under £5
Tel: 01904 654818
Disabled access: full
Other facilities: exhibitions,
conferences, functions and dinners

Micklegate Bar
Micklegate; map B6

This bar was where kings, queens and princes entered the city from the south and so was York's most important gateway. It is also an access point for the highest part of the Bar Walls. There is a small museum housed within the bar itself, which offers an insight into the history of the city, and includes information about the traitors whose heads were once displayed at the bar.
Museum Open: Feb–Oct: daily 9.00–17.00; Nov–Feb: Sat–Sun 9.00–dusk **Entry:** under £5
Tel: 01904 634436
Website: www.micklegatebar.co.uk
Disabled access: none

Monk Bar
Goodramgate; map F2

Monk Bar, the tallest of York's fine and famous city gates, spans Goodramgate in the north-east section of the wall. Carved figureheads on the top of the towers hold stones to drop on the enemy below – medieval invaders could have expected boiling tar as well! There are many surviving artefacts in its three storeys, including a portcullis which still works. In its upper floor is the Richard III Museum (see page 46).
Open: daily; Apr–Oct: 9.00–17.00; Nov–Mar: 9.30–16.00
Entry: under £5
Tel: 01904 634191
Disabled access: none

Monk Bar

Micklegate Bar

Multangular Tower
Museum Gardens; map C2

York's Roman fortress was surrounded by a fortified wall. The Multangular Tower, built in AD 300, is almost all that is left of these historic defences. It stands in Museum Gardens, close to the Yorkshire Museum and a short distance west of the Minster.

Open: daily; summer 8.00–20.00; winter 8.00–17.30
Entry: free
Disabled access: limited

the medieval Hospitium housed the abbey's guests. Lendal Tower was built in the 14th century as part of the city defences, but became York's first water-works in 1682, using water pumped from the river. An observatory in the park, built in 1833, fell out of favour when the lights of the city made star-gazing in central York a fruitless pursuit.

Open: daily; summer 8.00–20.00; winter 8.00–17.30
Entry: free
Disabled access: full

Multangular Tower

Museum Gardens
map B2/3–C2/3

This large and lovely park provides ample opportunities to wander, to sit amongst darting squirrels, or to feed appreciative ducks from the nearby River Ouse. It contains not only the Yorkshire Museum (see page 55) but historic features from a number of eras. The Multangular and the Anglian towers nearby are the main remnants of the Roman garrison walls. St Mary's Abbey (see page 47), now a graceful ruin, was once one of the wealthiest religious houses in Britain. Below it, by the river,

Museum Gardens

National Railway Museum

MALLARD

National Railway Museum
Leeman Road; map off A3

This is the finest collection of locomotives and trains in the country – perhaps in the world – all in beautiful condition and superbly displayed. The whole story of the train is here, from the primitive puffers of 1825, via *Mallard*, the fastest steam loco in the world, to the record-breaking Japanese Bullet Train. Besides the exhibits, there are interactive displays, daily demonstrations, video shows and many exciting children's activities.

DON'T MISS
Mallard, the streamlined locomotive that in 1938 achieved a never-beaten record speed for steam of 201 kph (126 mph).
The Japanese Bullet Train.
The inner secrets of a steam locomotive, revealed in a cutaway of 35029 Ellerman Lines.
Queen Victoria's royal saloon.
The workshops which show how a real signal box works.
The warehouse, the NRM's amazing reserve collection of railway memorabilia.
The winding engines, which spring into life several times a day, a reminder of the awesome power of steam.

Getting there: Less than 10 minutes down Leeman Road from York railway station, or by road train from the Minster (Apr–Oct)
Open: daily; 10.00–18.00. Closed 24–26 Dec only
Entry: free
Tel: 01904 621261
Website: www.nrm.org.uk
Disabled: limited
Other facilities: restaurant, gift shop and library

Newgate Market

Newgate Market

Parliament Street; map E4

Yorkshire's only seven-day open market.
Just the place for bargain hunters, with
over 100 stalls selling clothes, crafts
and gifts, as well as fruit and vegetables.
This colourful, typically English scene
is even more magical under the festive
Christmas lights.

Open: daily
Entry: free
Tel: 01904 551355
Disabled access: full

BATTLE WITH THE MOTOR CAR

To the horror of many, a new
street, Deangate, was driven
through medieval houses to
the south of the Minster in
1903 so that the wealthy could
reach the cathedral in their
new-fangled motor cars. In
1990, public pressure forced its
permanent closure to traffic.

Our Lady Row

Our Lady Row
Goodramgate; map F3
Our Lady Row, in front of Holy Trinity churchyard, was built in 1316 and is the oldest surviving row of houses in the city. Thomas Langtoft, a wealthy merchant, built them so that the ensuing rent would pay for a chantry priest at nearby Holy Trinity to say masses for his soul. Two storeys up and one room deep, the cottages (now shops) provide a very early example of 'jettying', where the upper storey projects outwards.

Parliament Street
map E4
The heart of York's shopping area, Parliament Street is the focus for special outdoor events. All vehicles are banished during the day, giving way to street musicians, circus performers, street theatre and pavement games in summer, and specialist markets and fairs at other times in the year.

Red House
1 Duncombe Place; map D2
If you like antiques, this is the place for you. Red House is an elegant, Queen Anne house at the corner of Duncombe Place and St Leonard's Place, built 1702–4, and once the home of a former Lord Mayor and MP. These days, over 60 antique dealers sell their wares here.
Open: Mon-Fri 9.30–17.30, Sat 9.30–18.00, Sun 10.30–17.30
Entry: free
Tel: 01904 637000
Website: www.redhouseyork.co.uk
Disabled access: none
Other facilities: café and bar

GRISLY HEADS
In Shakespeare's *Henry VI*, Queen Margaret orders the head of Richard Duke of York to be set on one of the gates of York 'that York may overlook the town of York'. The practice of displaying the heads of traitors on the city bars continued until 1752.

Parliament Street

Red House

Richard III Museum
Monk Bar, Goodramgate; map F2

In an atmospheric room over Monk Bar, you'll be able to read all sorts of quirky, offbeat facts, not only about the infamous hunchback king but also about royalty in general. This is your chance to check out a medieval loo, work the portcullis mechanism, and lock yourself in a cell! You can also spend a candlelit evening with His Majesty (see page 80). Sophisticated it's not, but it's certainly fun.

Open: daily; Mar–Oct: 9.00–17.00; Nov–Feb: 9.30–16.00
Entry: under £5
Tel: 01904 634191
Website: www. richard3museum.co.uk
Disabled access: none

St Helen's Square

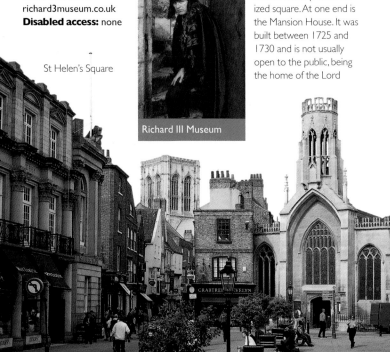

Richard III Museum

RICHARD THE GOOD

Richard III is vilified by Shakespeare and by most historians as the man who seized the throne by murdering Henry VI and his two sons. But in York he is respected as a capable administrator of the region, as well as a great benefactor to the Minster.

St Helen's Square
map D3

Five streets descend on this attractive pedestrianized square. At one end is the Mansion House. It was built between 1725 and 1730 and is not usually open to the public, being the home of the Lord

CRABTREE & EVELYN

Mayor. You can see the city's coat of arms in the pediment at the top of the building. At the other end of the square is St Helen's Church, and in between are Betty's famous tearooms and the site of Joseph Terry's original chocolate shop.

St Martin Le Grand
Coney Street; map D4

This mainly 15th-century church is readily located by its large clock which juts out into Coney Street. Reconciliation is a major theme here, for the church was severely damaged in the air raids of 1942 and, as a result, its organ was a gift from the German government.
Open: Mon–Fri 9.00–17.00
Entry: free
Tel: 01904 625186
Disabled access: full, but please phone first

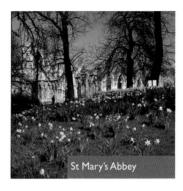

St Mary's Abbey

St Martin Le Grand's distinctive clock

St Mary's Abbey
Museum Gardens; map C2

Next to the Yorkshire Museum (see page 55) are the evocative ruins of what was once the wealthiest Benedictine monastery in the northern England. As with so many of England's fine abbeys, it fell victim to Henry VIII's dissolution, its stones being used to build the County Gaol and the Ouse Bridge. Nevertheless, the elegant walls that survive offer a romantic and peaceful setting for an interlude in sightseeing.
Open: daily; summer 8.00–20.00; winter 8.00–17.30
Entry: free
Disabled access: limited

St William's College
College Street; map E2/F2

This fine Tudor building stands in the shadow of the Minster. It was built in the 1460s to house the Minster's chantry priests, but in subsequent years it has been used for many things – including the Royal Mint and printing house for Charles I during

the Civil War. Now it houses a restaurant, which is also open in the morning for coffee and snacks. Three other spectacular medieval rooms are open to the public for a small admission charge.
Open: Mon–Sat 9.00–17.00, Sun 10.00–17.00 (subject to functions)
Entry: free to patrons, under £5 to visit other medieval rooms
Tel: 01904 557233
Website: www.yorkminster.org
Disabled access: none
Facilities: restaurant, exhibition and conference centre

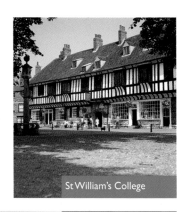
St William's College

The Shambles
map F4
This beautifully preserved medieval street is probably the most famous of its kind in Britain. Here, jettied, half-timbered buildings lean precariously into a narrow, winding, cobbled lane, which used to be home to dozens of butchers' shops – 'shammels' were the shelves on which the meat was displayed – and the narrowness was deliberate to keep the sun off the meat. The butchers have long gone, to be replaced by gift shops and delis, but much of the medieval magic still remains.

The good news is there's a wonderful bread shop in the Shambles. The bad news is you have to get there early before they sell out! Look out also for the chocolate shop and the heraldic art shop.

MARGARET CLITHEROW
In the Shambles is a shrine to Margaret Clitherow, the first woman in England to be martyred for her faith. A Roman Catholic convert, she repeatedly hid priests at a time when Catholic worship was outlawed. She was executed at Ouse Bridge in 1586.

Stonegate
map D3
This charming stone-paved shopping street has been a thoroughfare for nearly 2,000 years. No doubt the young Emperor Constantine travelled this way en route back to Rome from his coronation in York. The buildings represent a

variety of styles and ages, integrated into a delightful whole. Look out for Ye Olde Starre Inne, reputed to be the oldest alehouse in York, in an alleyway just off the street. Don't forget to go back there at night to sample the magic. There are some excellent tearooms here as well: Beams lives up to its name, and Little Betty's is every bit as good as its big sister in St Helen's Square.

Theatre Royal
St Leonard's Place; map D2
Appearances can be deceptive. The foyer may be modern plate glass, and the main shell may look like a Victorian public hall, but inside is a charming Georgian theatre with a traditional feel to it. The theatre has a reputation for high-class productions, both from touring companies and from local drama groups. There is also more intimate theatre in the Studio plus a plentiful helping of one-off shows of all types throughout the year. Worth checking what's on before you arrive.
Box office open: Mon 10.00–18.00, Tue–Sat 10.00–20.00
Tel: 01904 623568
Website: www.yorktheatreroyal.co.uk
Disabled access: full
Other facilities: café/bar

Treasurer's House
Minster Yard; map E1
This 17th-century National Trust town house is one of York's hidden treasures, tucked away behind the Minster. In an early version of the television programme *Changing Rooms*, its then owner, industrialist Frank Green, created

The Golden Slipper, Goodramgate

FAMOUS OLD BOY
Guy Fawkes of Gunpowder Plot fame was born in Stonegate. St Peter's School, York, has a bonfire on 5 November but never burns an effigy of Guy Fawkes – he's an ex-pupil!

Treasurer's House

13 rooms decorated and furnished in the style of four different centuries! The house, now owned by The National Trust, contains a wealth of art, pottery and textiles and is often host to exhibitions and special interest days. If you want a quiet few minutes, Treasurer's House has a delightful walled garden.

Open: end Mar–end Oct: Sat–Thu 11.00–16.30

Entry: under £5

Tel: 01904 624247

Disabled access: limited, but please phone first

Facilities: art gallery, tearoom and baby changing facilities

Walls
see Bar Walls

Walmgate Bar
Barbican Road
This bar is off the main tourist beat, but worth a walk to see the barbican (the outer fortification and gateway). Walmgate Bar is the only city gate in Britain to have retained its barbican. During England's Civil War (1642–5) York was a Royalist stronghold, and you don't have to look too closely to see the damage done by Oliver Cromwell's guns in 1644.

Getting there: a 10-minute walk down Fossgate

York Brewery Tour
Toft Green; map B5
York Brewery is a friendly, independent brewery, established in 1996, which

brews real ale, that is, beer brewed traditionally, conditioned in the cask, and
served by hand pump. Justifiably proud
of their product, the brewery invites
visitors to see and smell the beer being
brewed, and later taste the results.
Open: Mon–Sat; tours at 12.30, 14.00,
15.30, 17.00
Entry: under £5
Tel: 01904 621162
Website: www.yorkbrew.co.uk
Disabled access: limited
Other facilities: bar and shop

York City Art Gallery
Exhibition Square; map
C1/C2

The gallery contains a
fine collection of
European and British
paintings from several
centuries. Don't miss
the special collection
of views of York
seen through the
eyes of artists over
the last 300 years.
Open: daily
10.00–17.00
Entry: free
Tel: 01904 687687
Disabled access: full
Other facilities: shop

York Dungeon
Clifford Street; map E5
York's rich history is long, fascinating –
and bloody. York Dungeon's mission is to
bring you all the gory bits in loving and
lifelike detail – 'glorious Technicolor', you
might say. Go pillaging with the Vikings in

Jorvik, visit the torture chamber where
Guy Fawkes is getting the treatment,
watch Dick Turpin swing gently from the
gallows. Strictly for the non-squeamish!
Open: daily 10.30–17.00
Entry: under £10
Tel: 01904 632599
Website: www.thedungeons.com
Disabled access: limited, except for
the widest wheelchairs

York Model Railway Museum

York Model Railway Museum
York Station; map A4
The largest of the three railway layouts
has nearly a kilometre (half a mile) of
track, with up to 18 trains running at
the push of an interactive button. Look
out for many realistic but often wacky
features: a fairground, a hippy camp and
visitors from other worlds. The Thomas
the Tank Engine layout is very popular.
Open: daily; Mar–Oct: 9.00–18.00;
Nov–Feb: 10.00–17.00
Entry: under £5
Tel: 01904 630169
Disabled access: full, except for the
widest wheelchairs

York Minster
map E2

York Minster dominates the city, emerging grandly from the huddle of ancient streets and houses around. It's the north of England's main cathedral, and the largest medieval Gothic church north of the Alps. It is particularly famous for its beautiful and ancient stained-glass windows. Amongst the Minster's many other treasures are choir stalls that are a stunning display of the woodcarver's art.

T R U N C A T E D   T O W E R
The Minster's Lantern Tower was not meant to stand on its own. It was designed to be the platform for a belfry and spire, but when the tower began to crack, plans for the bell tower and spire were abandoned.

Chapter House roof   The rose window

History

The Minster was built 1220–1472 in the Gothic style, identified by the many pointed windows and arches. Archbishop Walter Gray's aim was that York's new church should rival that of Canterbury. The shape of the building has altered little in 800 years, but disaster has struck several times. In 1407 the tower partially collapsed, putting an end to plans for a grand belfry and spire. The 19th century saw two major fires, one in 1829 destroying the choir stalls, the other in 1840 the nave roof. In 1984 a third fire destroyed the south transept roof. Through all this, with the help of donations, generations of craftsmen have each time brought the Minster back to its full glory.

DON'T MISS

1 The west window, known as the 'heart of Yorkshire'.
2 The medieval glass windows on either side of the nave – some of the oldest stained glass in England.
3 The 'Five Sisters' window in the north transept. Completed in 1250, this very

The Minster's nave

world, as large as a tennis court!

9 The south transept. Restored after the fire of 1984, it contains the famous rose window, and some lovely modern roof bosses.

10 The Undercroft, Crypt and Treasury. A marvellous audio tour takes you on a time trip through the Minster's history.

early example contains over 100,000 pieces of grisaille glass.

4 The Chapter House. Don't miss the exquisite faces and beasts hiding in the stonework.

5 The Lantern Tower. Gaze upwards from near the choir screen.

6 The beautifully carved choir stalls, which were completely rebuilt after the fire of 1829.

7 The 17th-century painted monuments in the north and south nave aisles.

8 The great east window – the largest area of medieval stained glass in the

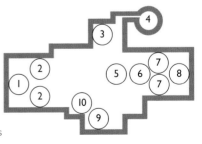

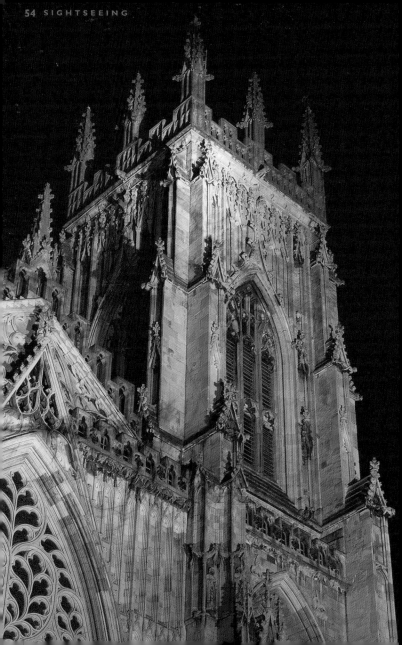

And if you have more time, why not
… spend a while sitting quietly in the
Zouche Chapel or crypt.
… climb the central tower. It's a 275-step
journey which is not for the faint-hearted
or the claustrophobic, but the view from
the top on a clear day is stunning.
Open: daily for services 7.00; for visitors: Mon–Sat 9.00–16.45,
Sun 12.30–15.45. Opening times
subject to services. Please ring to check
Entry: under £5
Tel: 01904 557216
Website: www.yorkminster.org
Disabled access: limited
Other facilities: shop

Yorkshire Museum

Yorkshire Air Museum
Elvington
Step back in time to life on a bomber
command station of World War II.
Fascinating displays in original buildings
show you what it was like to be at the
sharp end in wartime. You'll also see
historic aircraft from the pioneering days
through to modern jets, including the
world's only restored Handley Page
Halifax bomber.
Getting there: Elvington is 5 miles
south-east of York, on the B1228

Open: daily; summer 10.00–17.00;
winter: 10.00–15.30. Closed 25–26 Dec
and 1 Jan
Entry: under £5
Tel: 01904 608595
Website: yorkshireairmuseum.co.uk
Disabled access: limited
Other facilities: café and shop

Yorkshire Museum
Museum Gardens; map C2
Two thousand years of Yorkshire's rich
heritage are on display a stone's throw
from the west end of the Minster. Set
in delightful gardens (see page 41), the
museum contains exhibits which include
fossilized dinosaurs and the exquisite
Middleham Jewel. The museum is
renowned for its special exhibitions.
Open: daily; 10.00–17.00. Closed
25–26 Dec and 1 Jan
Entry: under £5
Tel: 01904 687687
Website:
www.yorkshiremuseum.org.uk
Disabled access: full

Yorkshire Air Museum

Bar Walls

Dean's Park

BREATHING SPACE

York may be a city which oozes life but within its busy centre there are plenty of spots to spend a quiet few minutes and watch the world go by.

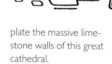

Museum Gardens;
map B2/3–C2/3
This is the place for duck-feeding and people-watching – acres of grass and plenty of seats. The ruins of St Mary's Abbey (see page 47) are particularly restful.

Dean's Park;
map D2–E2
Here, by the Minster, is a place where you can sit peacefully and contem-plate the massive lime-stone walls of this great cathedral.

Holy Trinity Church;
map E3
Not far from the east end of the Minster, a much humbler church off busy Goodramgate is a green haven of tranquillity. You can rest undisturbed in the churchyard but, if it's really hot, you can cool off in the church's dark and ancient interior (see page 36).

Bar Walls;
map D1–F1
Along the wall between Monk Bar and Bootham Bar are turrets with seats where you can either enjoy the peaceful gardens behind the Minster, or watch the hustle and bustle in the street on the other side of the wall.

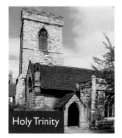
Holy Trinity

ARCHBISHOP'S PALACE
The Minster Library in Dean's Park is almost all that is left of the 13th-century Archbishop's Palace. The future Richard III was based in York as his brother's lieutenant in the north. It is at the palace in 1483 that Richard invested his son Edward as Prince of Wales.

City Screen, Coney Street;
map D4

City Screen is an excellent place to watch the river and have a quiet cuppa at the same time. This new venue is far more than an excellent cinema. It's a striking, modernistic café-bar, with a superb terrace overlooking the river. Open from 11.00.

Memorial Gardens;
map B3

Just over Lendal Bridge from the city centre is the Cenotaph, York's war memorial – designed, like its London counterpart, by Sir Edwin Lutyens. The gardens that surround it provide a peaceful spot to sit, savour the roses and watch the river.

St George's Gardens;
map E6

This is another peaceful riverside spot, with trees for shade. In summer you'll see an armada of narrow-boats, cruisers, tour boats – and plenty of geese.

The river

A pleasant stroll is to go upstream from Lendal Bridge (map C3). Cross the Scarborough railway/footbridge and come back on the other side. Alternatively go downstream from Ouse Bridge (map D5). On the other hand, you could always take a boat cruise for an hour or so (see page 83).

King's Staith on the River Ouse

York may be a historic city, but it offers some of the most cosmopolitan shopping streets in England – a day's treat for dedicated shoppers, while even resolute non-shoppers will find something of interest. Here is a quick rundown of the main shopping streets, followed by a selection of different kinds of shops.

SHOPPING

Opening hours
Most shops in York are open seven days a week, although Sunday hours are more limited – usually 11.00 to 17.00.

SHOPPING BY AREA
Coney Street, Spurriergate and Parliament Street; map D4 and E4

These are York's main shopping arteries, running parallel through the heart of the city. Here you will find the main, nationally known high street shops together with a few key independents.

Coppergate; map E4–F5
This street has good-quality high street shops and two excellent galleries.

Stonegate and Petergate; map D3 and D2–E3
These two ancient shopping streets are packed with a variety of high-class, independently owned shops. Stonegate particularly has jewellers, cook shops, glass and china, clothes and gifts, with Internet exchanges and plentiful tearooms thrown in. Petergate is even more

Andrea Bambridge Gowns, Goodramgate

varied: designer clothes, oodles of gifts, still more cafés, individual galleries, dolls and teddies. Look out for Scott's the pork butchers – there aren't many like this any more.

The Quarter; map E3
This hidden area comprising Little Stonegate, Back Swinegate and Grape Lane, has shrugged off its past as York's pig market and red-light district to become a mecca of independently owned designer boutiques, individual gift shops, cafés and wine bars.

Goodramgate; map F2–F3
Some very ordinary shops mixed with specialist gems which make the walk worthwhile. Look out for beer, sweets, chocolates, games and models.

Gillygate; map D1
Alternative shoppers' paradise – 20 or so charming little places, including interior design, music, clothing, wacky stuff and a vegetarian eatery.

Porcupine, Swinegate

TREAT YOURSELF
Buy yourself some exquisite soap or a fancy face-wash at Lush in Coney Street (map D4). All their soap is made from unusual natural ingredients, and is cut and weighed to your requirements. Even if you buy nothing, you can enjoy the wonderful, perfumed aromas.

Newgate Market; map E4
A traditional English market, open virtually all year round.

The Shambles; map F4
Quirky boutiques, cafés, heraldic art, chocolate and brilliant bread.

Fossgate; map F4–F5
Once known as Tricksters' Lane after its unscrupulous traders, but rest assured things have improved! Down here you'll find books, antiques, some fashion and a dolls' house shop, as well as some good restaurants.

Micklegate; map B6–D5
Over the river, but not to be overlooked. Up the hill there is an interesting mixture of bookshops, antique shops and good-value alternative cafés in a

McArthur Glen Designer Outlet

gentle crescent of 18th-century town houses.

Out of town
McArthur Glen Designer Outlet
Off the A64 ring road on the A19 towards Selby
Over 100 designer shops under one (enormous) roof – everything from Armani Blazer to Warner Brothers Studio Store, and with big discounts.
Getting there: by Redline

Park and Ride shuttle bus from the railway station every 15 minutes

Clifton Moor and Monks Cross
These are both just off the outer ring road (see small map on page 98), and are more orthodox centres, covering between them most of the big names you'd expect at an out-of-town location.

SELECTED SHOPS

High Street shops
If you start off from St Helen's Square (map D3) you won't go far wrong. South from here on parallel streets Davygate, and especially Coney Street, you'll find all the big names. The 'names' continue in Parliament Street and Spurriergate,

Micklegate

which in turn lead to Coppergate (near Jorvik).

Brown's
Davygate; map D3
A special word for Brown's, York's only independent department store, which is in one of the city's finest listed buildings on Davygate. Brown's is part of the city's history, having evolved from a small drapery shop into a thriving, modern store.

Gifts
York's popularity with visitors means that there are more high-quality gift shops than you can shake a stick at. Don't forget the many museum shops too.

Castle Museum shop; map F6
This has many interesting, nostalgic items.

Minster shop; map E2
Good for books, cards and high quality gifts.

Petergate; map D2–E3
Gift shops in Petergate include Christmas Angels and Cat Gallery (if you like cats!)

The Shambles; map F4
If you want something very individual, call in at Freeborn & Son in the Shambles. Although these craftsmen in wood concentrate on furniture, they also produce delight-

ful small gifts. Look out for the wooden apple with the mouse inside it.

Cat Gallery

Christmas Angels

Impressions Gallery

Halo

Arts and crafts
**Coppergate Walk;
map D4–F5**
Galleries here include
Impressions, one of the
country's leading photo-
graphic galleries, and
Castle Gallery with a
strong display of paintings
and prints. Elsewhere the
Japanese Print Shop in
Petergate (map D2), Porta
Dextra in The Quarter
(map E3) and Halo in
Gillygate (D1) are also
good for delightful gifts.

Clothes shops
For clothes, you can
choose between the city
centre or out-of-town
outlets. For independently
owned, city-centre shops,
head for Stonegate,
Petergate or the Quarter.

**Chinelli
Grape Lane; map E3**
Italian shoes for men and
women, with a few hand-
bags as well.

**Little Mill Shops
The Shambles; map F4**
Come here for clothes
that are woolly, warm
and attractive.

**McArthur Glen Designer
Outlet**
Ten minutes out of the
city on the south side, this
outlet (see page 61) offers
a huge variety of designer
shops. Just to drop a few
names: Armani, Burberry,
Dolce & Gabbana, Pringle,
Tommy Hilfiger – you get
the picture.

> **FREE VIEW**
> A free treat lies literally in store
> at Marks and Spencer (the branch at the
> corner of Parliament Street and Pavement).
> Take the escalator to the menswear depart-
> ment on the top floor, and find the window
> which looks out over the rooftops to the
> Minster. A telescope is even kindly
> provided.

Sarah Coggles

Humpty Dumpty

Priestley's Vintage Clothing
off Grape Lane; map E3
Immaculately presented clothes, accessories and fabrics for women and men, from the 1920s to the 1970s.

Sarah Coggles
Petergate; map E2
Lively and trendy.

Ten Thousand Men
Swinegate; map E3
Smart clothes for men.

Yo-Yo
Swinegate; map E3
Continental clothes for women.

Children's clothes
Humpty Dumpty
Stonegate; map D3
Unusual and individually designed clothes for children.

Moo
Gillygate; map D1
Funky, designer clothes for kids.

Food
Bread
The Shambles; map F4
Close to Newgate Market is Via Vecchia, a superb bread shop in the Shambles, but get there early – it's almost always sold out by lunchtime.

Health food
Colliergate; map F3
You'll find the staff in Tulliver's are both helpful and knowledgeable about their produce.

Via Vecchia (page 65)

Scott's the Pork Butchers

Henshelwoods Delicatessen

Newgate Market
Parliament Street; map E4
The market (see page 43) has a vast range of food stalls. Cross's fish stall has been a regular feature for many years. Nearby Henshelwoods Delicatessen produces lots of home-made goodies and boasts the best selection of cheese in Yorkshire.

Scott's the Pork Butchers
Low Petergate; map E3
Scott's has been established for over 100 years and produces some

mouth-watering meat specialities, including York hams, sausages and pork pies. It's not just pork though. Chicken parcels stuffed with Stilton and wrapped in bacon are a particular winner. Many a guest house fridge is packed with Scott's produce, waiting to be taken back home!

Homes and gardens
Antiques
Red House
1 Duncombe Place; map D2
Top of the list for antiques is the Red House. The rooms of this fine Georgian house (see page 44) are filled with lovely pieces, large and small, each room representing a

Red House

different era. No repro stuff here!

Stonegate Antiques
Stonegate; map D3
Stonegate Antiques comprises two attractive shops under the same management, focussing on smaller items, such as jewellery and pottery.

York Antiques Centre
Lendal; map D3
Two floors of antiques and collectables.

Micklegate; map B6–D5
This street has some good antiques shops, notably The French House.

China and glass
Mulberry Hall
Stonegate; map D3
Mulberry Hall on Stonegate is an outstanding china, glass and cookware shop set in a beautifully preserved medieval building. The firm boasts that their expert packers can despatch goods, trouble-free, to any part of the world.

China-China
McArthur Glen Designer Outlet
Less glamorous, but big and superb value.

Barnitts
Colliergate; map F3
Barnitts is a well-stocked shop selling all sorts of hardware, gardening, DIY and electrical goods.

Internet cafés
A complete list of Internet cafés in York and else-

where in the UK is available at www. netcafeguide.com. These are just two easy-to-find places in the centre of the city, from which you can keep in touch with the folks back home.

Gateway Internet Café
Coney Street; map D4

Evil Eye Lounge
Stonegate; map D3

Jewellery
Colliergate; map F3
Azendi is a recent, trendy shop.

Goodramgate; map F2
Asquith's of York has a range of jewellery, earrings being a particular feature. The shop is also a

Gateway Internet Café

manufacturing jewellers taking commissions, so order your personalized tiara now!

High Petergate; map D2
Foster's offers jewellery and silverware, antique and modern.

The Shambles; map F4
Silverado, as its name implies, focuses on items made in sterling silver.

Other specialist shops
Chocolate
Monk Bar (map F2) and the Shambles (map F4)
If only we could translate into print the gorgeous smell of Monk Bar Chocolatiers! They sell their own special chocolates at Monk Bar and also at Chocolate Heaven in the Shambles.

Low Petergate; map E3
Long-established Maxwell & Kennedy make their own chocolates from the best Belgian ingredients.

Dolls' houses
Fossgate; map F4
The Miniature Scene boasts that it is Britain's biggest and best dolls' house shop, with over 60 residences on display and a full range of materials to build one or furniture to equip it.

Embroidery and Knitting
The Shambles; map F4
Woolfayre sells wonderful wool and every conceivable accessory for the needleperson, knitter and rugmaker.

High Petergate; map D2
The Viking Loom in High

CHOCOLATE TOWN

Modern York was partially built of chocolate! In the 1900s there were around 20 confectioners. In the early 20th century, the chocolate industry was the second biggest employer after the railways, the two big firms being Terry's (now closed) and Rowntrees (now part of the Nestlé group).

Monk Bar Chocolatiers

Petergate caters for a wide range of crafty activities, including paper-craft, rubber stamping and patchwork.

Games
Goodramgate; map F2
Compendium of York near Monk Bar is totally devoted to traditional games, but you will also find shops selling other, computer-orientated games nearby.

Heraldry
The Shambles; map F4
Heraldic Art & Design will create an embroidered or calligraphic family crest for you, while along the lane Something Different will, amongst other heraldic things, provide you with the history of your surname, and perhaps sell you a reproduction sword or two.

Toys
Gillygate; map D1
Moo is an exciting hands-on experience for children, selling all manner of toys, puzzles, cuddlies, clothing – you name it. If it's cuddlies you're after, try the highly attractive Stonegate Teddy Bears in Stonegate (map D3).

The Chocolate Store, Goodramgate

Compendium of York

EATING AND DRINKING

Rish (page 78)

One thing is certain about your visit to York – you're not likely to go hungry! Wherever you stay, you're almost certain to be offered a full English breakfast, so you can fill yourself up at the start of the day with bacon, eggs, sausage, mushrooms, tomatoes and fried bread. Just remember, before you tuck in too lavishly, that York has a plethora of wonderful places to lunch, to dine, and for plenty of little fillers in between! Here are a few suggestions for places which enjoy a reputation for great food. Whatever your taste you should find something to tickle your palate. And whichever you choose, *bon appétit!*

CAFES AND TEAROOMS

You can hardly go wrong amid York's café culture. Almost everywhere, a few strides will take you to a comfortable place to while away some time with a tea, a coffee or a bite to eat. These are some of the most popular.

Ambience
Gillygate; map D1
Includes a garden and a working clockmakers. Good for families or long lunches. Burgers a speciality.

Bar Convent
Blossom Street; map B6
City-centre hideaway (see also page 32), tracked down mainly by older people and business folk. Good value jacket potatoes, baguettes and salads, plus specials.

Betty's Café Tearooms
St Helen's Square; map D3
York's favourite traditional tearooms with an art deco interior inspired by the founder's trip on the *Queen Mary* in 1936. A reviewer described Betty's as the sort of place that Jeeves and Wooster would have enjoyed. Trendy it certainly isn't,

Betty's

LUCKY ACCIDENT

Betty's Tearooms were established in Harrogate in 1919. The founder, Frederick Belmont, came from Switzerland, accidentally caught the wrong train in London and ended up in Yorkshire. As it reminded him of his native Alps, he stayed. The rest, as they say, is history.

but most visitors consider that traditional afternoon tea at Betty's is unmissable (see page 12). If you're disabled, wheelchair access planks tend to appear instantly, on request.

City Screen
Coney Street; map D4
Café-bar for late morning coffee or a bite later on. Plate glass and steel, with comfy leather seats and overlooking the river. Generous faux-rustic cuisine – anyone for wild boar sausages or balsamic baked mushrooms? Open pub hours. You can take in a film or simply enjoy the wonderful view.

Delifrance
Low Petergate; map E3
Simple, family place with beams and city views upstairs. As the name suggests, it's French food that's on offer here. You can kick off with a continental breakfast, or sample lunch from a menu that includes home-baked baguettes, croissants and pastries together with fillings and salad. And there's a licensed bar.

Gateway Internet Café Bar
Coney Street; map D4
A compact place full of trendy iMacs. Simple screen-staring fodder – hot chocolate, baguettes, soup, sandwiches – while you bash away at the keyboard. And a licensed bar as well.

City Screen

Little Betty's
Stonegate; map D3
Less well-known, but
prides itself on being just

Little Betty's

as good as 'big sister', in a
cosier, medieval setting.

Pitcher and Piano
Coney Street; map D4
Popular café-bar with river
view. Flashy steel, glass and
pine plus good service
and appetizing food.
Packed on race days.

Spurriergate Centre
Spurriergate; map E4
Converted historic church
which serves good-value,
wholesome food in a
village fête atmosphere.

RESTAURANTS
Bistros
Café Concerto
High Petergate; map D2
The place to unwind with
a bottle of wine as you
saunter through an

eclectic, mid-priced menu.
Atmospheric and very
popular with local people.
Tel: 01904 610478

Meltons Too
Walmgate
How to define the indefin-
able! Multicultural mid-

Café Concerto

priced eating in a relaxed, chic setting – modern feel in an ancient building. Pick-and-mix informal menu covers anything from traditional British to Thai, via Spain, North Africa and most other places.
Tel: 01904 62922

J. Bakers
Fossgate; map F4
A contemporary modern bistro serving simple but bold, familiar but new food in a relaxing environment run by Michelin Star chef Jeff Baker.
Tel: 01904 622688

British
Middlethorpe Hall
Bishopthorpe Road
Where York's wealthy go for a tip-top meal in supremely elegant surroundings. Bask in the warm glow of a bygone age, but don't forget your smart clothes – or wallet.
Tel: 01904 641241

Russells
Stonegate; map D3 or Coppergate; map E5
There's nowhere better for a good old English roast at a reasonable price. If you go to the Coppergate branch, have a peep at the splendid room upstairs.
Tel: 01904 641432

St William's Restaurant

Jumbo Chinese Buffet

Fish
Blue Bicycle
Fossgate; map F4
Everyone speaks very
highly of this cosy, informal
restaurant. If you like
fish, this is definitely the
place to go – but almost
certainly you'll need to
book ahead.
Tel: 01904 673990

St William's Restaurant
College Street; map E2/F2
York Minster's own
licensed restaurant. Open-
air by day or candlelit by
night. Good home-made
meals in historic surroundings – English cuisine with
a dash of Mediterranean
tastes and ingredients.
Tel: 01904 634830

Chinese
Jumbo Chinese Buffet
George Hudson Street;
map C4
This popular, family restaurant is just off the main
tourist beat. It provides
all-you-can-eat for a set
price, and only the ultra-
greedy would need longer
than the permitted hour
and a half for three
Cantonese courses from
the vast selection of dishes
on offer.
Tel: 01904 623656

Petergate Fish and Chip
Shop

Wackers of York
Gillygate; map D1
Fish and chips in a
spacious restaurant not
far from Bootham Bar.
Tel: 01904 672279

Indian
Aagrah
York Road, Steeton near
Tadcaster
This award-winning, excel-
lent-value Indian is worth
the 7-mile trip along the
A64, especially if you have

Blue Bicycle

several mouths to feed. Dull outside, lavish within. Super choice of Kashmiri dishes, including many vegetarian options.
Tel: 01937 530888

Jaipur Spice
Haxby Road (near the Hospital)
Memorably grand in scale, the Jaipur Spice is popular with parties heading for an evening out. Good food, good prices and service.
Tel: 01904 673550

Italian
ASK
Blake Street; map D3
Not your average Italian restaurant this! Enjoy a romantic meal amongst the Palladian colonnades and palms in the 1735 Assembly Rooms (see page 30). The food is good

with both style and prices not as grand as the setting.
Tel: 01904 637254

Delrio's
Blossom Street; map A6
Relax in a warm, authentic Sardinian atmosphere. Traditional Italian food with the emphasis on fish, and plenty for vegetarians too.
Tel: 01904 622695

Villa Italia
Micklegate; map B6–D5
A popular, unpretentious place with cool marble decor. Good food at reasonable prices makes it very popular with those who know about it.
Tel: 01904 670501

Mexican
Fiesta Mehicana
Clifford Street; map E5
Absolutely Aztec. Totally

tortilla. Mucho mariachi. Two floors of fun, with friendly service and plenty of vegetarian options.
Tel: 01904 610243

Plunkets
High Petergate; map D2
Although the cooking is cosmopolitan, it is Tex-Mex that's especially popular. Medium priced, mega portions, hippy ambience. Particularly busy at weekends.
Tel: 01904 637722

Thai
Siam House Thai Restaurant
Goodramgate; map F2
Ceiling fans and bamboo-clad walls create a real Thai feel in this popular eating house. The chilli fish and green curries are particular favourites and there are veggie options. It's particularly packed in the evenings and at weekends, so advance booking is recommended.
Tel: 01904 624677

Vegetarian
El Piano
Grape Lane; map E3
Delicious smells will draw you into El Piano, which specializes in vegan

El Piano (page 77)

cooking in a Spanish-
Bohemian atmosphere.
Tel: 01904 610676

Greenhouse
Church Street; map E3
This is another restaurant
worth trying.
Tel: 01904 629615

The Blake Head
Vegetarian Cafe
Micklegate; map C5
Healthy but huge portions
of home-made veggie
food.
Tel: 01904 623767

See also Aagrah (page 76),
Delrio's, Fiesta Mehicana
and Siam House Thai
Restaurant (page 77).

PUBS
Last Drop Inn
Colliergate; map F3
Busy, friendly, city-centre
pub owned by York
Brewery. Traditionally
modern (or modernisti-
cally traditional), it's
refreshingly free of fruit
machines, jukeboxes and
other electronic distrac-
tions. And the beer's good
too. Frequent live music.

The Maltings
Tanners Moat; map C4
Smoky and poky but
packed with character
and good humour. Varied
beers expertly kept.
A genuine pub with a
capital P. It hosts folk and
blues nights each week.

Roman Bath
St Sampson's Square;
map E3
What makes this ordinary,

good-hearted pub special
is the Roman baths you
can ask to see in the
cellar. Generous, unpre-
tentious food and, in the
evenings, live music is
often provided.

Royal Oak
Goodramgate; map F2
Without doubt the first
place to go in York for
a pub lunch. An old-
fashioned community pub
in the heart of the city.
The beer's well kept and
the food well cooked.

Three Legged Mare
High Petergate; map D2
The owners (York
Brewery) pride them-
selves on an atmosphere
of mature conversation
uninterrupted by jukebox,
TV, children, and so on.
Jacket potatoes and
baguettes at lunchtime.

The Maltings

Snickleway Inn (page 81)

AN EVENING OUT

interesting, guided walks to be had (see page 83), as well as floodlit evening cruises (see page 83).

An evening with Richard III

On Fridays and Saturdays in July and August you can spend a candlelit evening with the infamous Richard III at the Monk Bar museum (map F2), which bears his name. Bring your own wine. You'll get his life history, the chance to ask him questions, and even enjoy a song.
Tel: 01904 634191

Deciding how to spend an evening in York is difficult. There are so many choices – from a simple night out at a pub to a full-dress night at the opera.

Ghost walks

What about a ghost walk around the most haunted city in Europe? Spooky walks start at several points in the city centre. Look out for the placards. The Ghost Hunt of York, tel: 01904 608700
Ghost Trail, tel: 01904 633276

The Original Ghost Walk of York, tel: 01759 373090 Alternatively, Yorkboat do an evening ghost cruise (tel: 01904 628324 for details).

Guided walks and floodlit cruises

There are also more conventional, but very

ANCIENT GHOSTS

A young plumber working in the cellars of Treasurer's House in 1953 was terrified to see a troop of ghostly Roman legionaries appéar through a wall. He described them in perfect detail. The house, it turned out, was built on the site of a Roman road.

Film and theatre

More orthodox entertainments include the splendid City Screen cinema (tel: 01904 541155 for information) and café-bar (see page 73), the Theatre Royal (see page 49), the Grand Opera House, Cumberland Street (tel: 01904 671818; map E5) and the Friargate Theatre, Friargate (tel: 0845 961 3000; map E5).

Classical music

During term time, orchestral and chamber concerts are held at York University's two principal halls (tel: 01904 432431 for details).

Pubs

If simpler things appeal to you then you could do worse than go along to The Maltings in Tanners Moat, near Lendal Bridge (map C4). On two nights a week there is folk and blues (the pub gets very smoky, though!).

The Black Swan at Peasholme Green has jazz and folk, too, on two nights a week.

The Snickleway Inn on Goodramgate (map F2) has considerable character and perhaps more – it is said to be the most haunted pub in the city.

Nightclub

If you've still got energy left, Toffs Nightclub (Toft Green, map B5) is open until the small hours (www.toffsnightclub.co.uk for further details).

The Maltings

Casa, Low Ousegate

TOURS AND TRIPS

There are all sorts of ways to see York by day and night. Because the city centre is compact and full of nooks and crannies where cars — mercifully — can't go, walking is undoubtedly the best way to get around. But that's not to say that other modes of transport won't add an extra something to your stay.

River cruise

Bar Walls

On foot
York is a pedestrian's paradise. Most of the city-centre streets are relatively free of traffic for much of the day. Besides that, there are medieval city walls, riverside paths and all the hidden snickel-ways to explore. Three walks are suggested on pages 24–29. Alternatively, York offers many superb guided walks by both day and night, all year round.

Free guided walks

Hosted by volunteer guides, walks leave regularly all year round from Exhibiton Square (map D2), opposite the Tourist Information Centre in the De Grey Rooms.
Times: summer 10.15, 14.15 and 18.45; winter 10.15

Themed walks

There are some excellent daytime themed walks led by professional guides. Cost is usually about £5.
Yorkwalk;

tel: 01904 622303
The Viking Walk;
tel: 07796 772001
Roam'in Tours;
tel: 01904 468857

By bike

York has a terrific network of cycle paths giving easy, safe access to all the major attractions in and beyond the city. How about enjoying a cycling picnic along the river?

By bus

Perhaps the best way to get your bearings quickly

in York is to take a round-the-city ride in an open-topped bus. Guide Friday and York City Sightseeing buses regularly leave from Exhibition Square (map D2) with many hop-on and hop-off points around the city. The full circuit takes around 40 minutes.
Tel: York City Sightseeing 01904 655585; Guide Friday 01904 655585

On the water

An even more relaxing way to see York is to take a boat cruise from King's Staith (map E5) or Lendal Bridge (map C3).

Yorkboat

Yorkboat do a variety of cruises at different times of the day and evening. They also hire out self-drive motor boats.
Tel: 01904 628324

Ghost walk

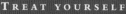

TREAT YOURSELF
Ever tasted Yorkshire Terrier or Centurion's Ghost? Sample these and other speciality ales after a tour round York's very own brewery. Tours are available daily. More details on page 50.

There's no excuse for having a dull time in York. Even in the winter season, the city hosts festivals and international events for all tastes and interests. Only the biggest events are listed here.

WHAT'S ON

YORK MYSTERY PLAYS
These feature scenes from the Old Testament and originated in the 14th century. They are traditionally performed in a four-year cycle, in 2004, 2008, etc. Venues vary – look on www.yorkearlymusic.org/mysteryplays/ for more information.

Jolablot

February
Jorvik Viking Festival 'Jolablot'
For a wild weekend, the city relives its Viking past, with raucous banquets, mock battles and longboat races on the Ouse. Danes once more settle in Coppergate, and hairy men in horned helmets wander the streets.
Tel: 01904 543403

May to October
York Races
Summer brings the flat racing season to the fine racecourse at Knavesmire (on the A1036 Tadcaster Road). Meetings each

month last several days, the highlight being the Ebor in August.
Tel: 01904 620911

June
National Cycle Rally
Cyclists of all types descend on the racecourse at Knavesmire. Events include grass-track racing, exhibitions, children's entertainment and the grand parade of over 1,000 bicycles through the city.

Street entertainment during the Early Music Festival in July

July
York Early Music Festival
York is privileged to have the National Centre for Early Music. Their ten-day summer festival may feature music from 7th-century plainsong up to around 1850. Performances take place in the Centre in St Margaret's on Walmgate, in York Minster and other historic churches in the city.
Tel: 01904 658338

September
Festival of Food and Drink
This annual event is the largest of its kind in the UK. For ten days in mid-September, food takes over the city, with specialist markets (based in Parliament Street and St Sampson's Square), themed dinners, product launches and celebrity chefs, plus a multitude of other special events.
Tel: 01904 554430

National Book Fair
This mammoth annual event sees York's Barbican Centre swamped by thousands of second-hand books from all over the country.
Tel: 01763 248400

November/December
St Nicholas Fayre
During late November and December, the city crackles with old-fash-ioned pre-Christmas atmosphere: a sparkling concoction of lights, Christmas trees and Victorian street stalls. In Parliament Street and St Sampson's Square you will find specialist craft and food markets. At the same time you can enjoy the street theatre, music and dance going on around.
Tel: 01904 554430

York Races

December
York Early Music Christmas Festival
Like its July counterpart, the festival is organized by the National Centre for Early Music, this time over a long weekend. As in summer there are vocal, orchestral and chamber concerts, most of them with a Christmas feel.
Tel: 01904 658338

York's an exciting place for children, full of enjoyment and education. They won't forget their visit to York.

YORK FOR KIDS

York Minster

York Minster (see pages 52–55) is a must. Take a minute to sit and look up into the Lantern Tower too. Find the *Blue Peter* roof bosses in the south transept. Children will also enjoy the glass in the nave aisles, the astronomical clock, the colourful monuments and the line of kings in the stone screen. The view from the tower is well worth the climb.

BLUE PETER BOSSES

In the 1984 fire, the roof of the Minster's south transept was destroyed. Six of the 68 new roof bosses (the ornamental knobs where the ceiling ribs cross) were designed by viewers of the popular TV programme *Blue Peter*.

Live-action history

Jorvik (see page 38) is another essential, unforgettably bringing the city's past to life. Pre-booking saves queuing!

Visit nearby DIG (see page 30) for some hands-on detective work, using real Viking and Roman artefacts.

Castle Museum

(see page 34) is a magical place for everyone. The Victorian street is the star attraction, but remember that there's a toy gallery and a working watermill later in the tour.

For railway enthusiasts

The National Railway Museum (see page 42) is a must for any mechanically-minded child. Start in the Great Hall with the *Rocket* replica, progressing

TREAT THE FAMILY

Treat yourself as well as the kids to an old-fashioned ice cream at the Mowbray shop and tearooms on Stonegate.

Castle Museum

York Model Railway Museum

via *Mallard* to the Bullet Train. Queen Victoria's saloon is worth seeing too, and there are countless items of interest stored in the Warehouse.

At the railway station is York Model Railway Museum (see page 51), which is large, interactive and full of humorous touches for young and old.

Walks

Walk at least one section of the Bar Walls if you can (page 32). Perhaps the most exciting section for children is the bit near the railway station (map B4). In the evening, join a ghost walk (see page 80).

Playgrounds

Homestead Park, Water End, Clifton, about 1.5 km (1 mile) from Bootham Bar. Attractive park with good play equipment.

Rowntree Park, Terry Avenue, about 1 km (0.5 mile) south of the Castle Museum, on the far bank of the River Ouse. Lots of play equipment and a café.

Maize Maze

One innovation that's very popular with families is the Maize Maze, near Grimston Bar Park and Ride (see page 95). The

Maize Maze

challenge is to find your way through sculpted sweetcorn to the central platform. The shape changes every year. Tel: 01904 415364

Places to eat

One fun, cheap idea when tummies are rumbling is to eat outside in King's Square (map E3/F3). You can choose from fish and chips, sweet and savoury crepes, and a great range of other food. Or you can have a picnic in one of the parks and gardens (see pages 56–57). Other child-friendly, reasonably priced places to eat include Ambience in Gillygate (map D1), Spurriergate Centre (map E4) and St William's College (map E2/F2). At El Piano (see page 77) you can take kids in as late as you like and they won't mind a bit.

OUT OF TOWN

The delights and fascinations of York may keep you firmly anchored within its walls, but don't forget the countryside around. Here are some suggestions that are all less than two hours away by car, train or bus.

Castle Howard

15 miles north east of York; near Malton, off the A64

Without doubt the number-one day out from York is to 18th-century Castle Howard, one of England's greatest stately homes. It is less than an hour from York by bus. Designed by the Renaissance architect Sir John Vanbrugh, the interior, adorned with priceless paintings, furniture and tapestries, matches the grandeur of the exterior. Outside, you can either wander

Castle Howard

through the delightful gardens – the rose garden is especially famous – or lose yourself in the vast parkland, with its temples, lakes and fountains.

Whitby and the Moors

45 miles north east of York; A64 to Malton then A169 to Whitby

The North York Moors are a wild and lovely upland area, covered with heather and riven by deep valleys. You can drive across the Moors from Pickering to Whitby, or take the steam train from Pickering to Grosmont. Further east the moors tumble dramatically into the sea. Two hours by bus from York will get you to the lovely fishing port of Whitby, home of explorer Captain Cook (don't forget to visit the Captain Cook Museum) and famous for its ruined clifftop abbey. Robin

TREAT YOURSELF
Take a trip on the Scarborough Spa Express, an hour's steam train excursion from York station to the famous Yorkshire seaside resort every Tuesday, Wednesday and Thursday throughout July and August.
Tel: 01524 732100
Website: www.britainexpress.com

Hood's Bay is typical of several lovely coastal villages nearby.

Yorkshire Dales
34 miles north west of York; A59 and A61 to Ripon

West from York lie the Yorkshire Dales, perhaps the most scenic and popular part of the Pennine uplands – the 'backbone of northern England'. Wharfedale and Wensleydale descend from austere limestone moorlands to become mellow, welcoming valleys with wandering streams, scattered woods and grazing sheep in neat fields picked out by dry-stone walls. Dotted about are unspoilt stone villages,

Knaresborough

many with excellent pubs and teashops. The two most visited places are Fountains Abbey, a romantic valley ruin, and the small cathedral city of Ripon nearby.

Harrogate and Knaresborough
18 miles west of York, A59

Harrogate is only half an hour away by train. This famous spa town retains an air of Victorian gentility, with broad streets and plentiful open space. The pace is leisurely, the shops are exclusive but expensive. The original Betty's tearooms are here too.

Nearby, Knaresborough is a quaint market town with many Georgian houses, and a castle perched on a crag overlooking the River Nidd. Harewood House, south of Harrogate, is also definitely worth visiting.

Whitby

WHERE TO STAY

Hotel 53 (page 92)

The Tourist Information Centre (see page 94) offers a friendly accommodation booking service in return for a small fee. They also publish a comprehensive guide to all types of accommodation, which you can send for in advance. The selection that follows will give you an idea of the range on offer. Check facilities and prices before you book.

Prices

The £ symbols are an approximate guide for comparing the prices charged, which range from about £25 to over £100 per person per night.

York Marriott
Tadcaster Road, York

A 108-bed hotel in beautiful grounds overlooking the racecourse. The hotel provides a courtesy bus to the centre of York, and includes extensive facilities such as an indoor pool, and sauna.
Tel: 01904 701000
Website: www.
marriotthotels.com/qqyyk
££££

Middlethorpe Hall
Bishopthorpe Road, York

A 30-bed, 17th-century house in parkland, 5 km (3 miles) from the centre. Luxury accommodation (spa, fitness centre, etc) and a good reputation for cuisine.

Middlethorpe Hall

Tel: 01904 641241
Website:
www.middlethorpe.com
££££

Monkbar Hotel
St Maurice's Road, York

An independently-owned, 99-bed, modern hotel overlooking the city walls in the centre. Restaurant.
Tel: 01904 638086
Website:
www.monkbarhotel.co.uk
£££

Mount Royale Hotel
The Mount, York

A 23-bed, William-IV, listed building, ten minutes' walk from the centre. Antique furniture and lovely garden. Open air pool, steam room.
Tel: 01904 628856
£££

Hotel 53
53 Piccadilly, York; map F5

100-bed, modern hotel on the fringe of the centre. Restaurant.
Tel: 01904 559000
Website:
www.qualityhotelyork.com
££

The Grange Hotel
1 Clifton, York

A 30-bed Regency

Monkbar Hotel

townhouse, ten minutes' walk from the centre. Luxurious en suite bedrooms. Three styles of restaurant to choose from. Tel: 01904 644744 Website: www. grangehotel.co.uk ££

**Farthings Hotel
5 Nunthorpe Avenue, York**
A nine-bed, comfortable, Victorian guest house for non-smokers, just ten minutes' walk from the city centre. Tel: 01904 653545 Website: www. farthingsyork.co.uk ££

**Alexander House
94 Bishopthorpe Road, York**
This Victorian town house has four beds and is much in demand, being just ten minutes' walk from the centre of the city.

Tel: 01904 625016 Website: www. alexanderhouseyork.co.uk ££

**The Bar Convent
Blossom Street, York; map B6**
Good value bed and breakfast set-up in a 1787 building which is still a convent (see page 32). Here you can get up as early as you like and have a do-it-yourself continental breakfast with provided ingredients. It's handy for the station, too. Closed Good Fri–Easter Mon and 20 Dec–1 Feb. Tel: 01904 464902 Website: www. bar-convent.org.uk £

(see page 32)

FAMOUS GUESTS
Two of the Brontë sisters, Charlotte and Anne, en route to the spa at Scarborough (Anne was ill and only had a few months to live) stayed at the George Inn, Coney Street in 1849.

USEFUL INFORMATION

USEFUL WEBSITES

Planning your stay:
The official website for visitors to York is **www.visityork.org**
Others include
www.thisisyork.co.uk
www.cityofyork.com

Local buses:
www.firstyork.co.uk
Local journeys by bus and rail: www.ukbus.co.uk

For disabled people: www.shopmobilityyork.org.uk
www.tourismforall.org.uk
www.york.gov.uk/outabout/disabled

TOURIST INFORMATION

Tourist Information Centres
De Grey Rooms,
Exhibition Square,
map D2
York Railway Station,
map A4
Extensive range of services, including accommodation booking, travel and information on events.
Tel: 01904 550099

Website:
www.visityork.org

What's On
Look for *What's on in York* and *York Visitor Guide.* The daily newspaper *This is York* provides listings too, as does Friday morning's edition of the *Yorkshire Post.*

Guided walks
The Ghost Hunt of York;
tel: 01904 608700
Ghost Trail:
tel: 01904 633276
The Original Ghost Walk of York; tel: 01759 373090
Yorkwalk;
tel: 01904 622303
The Snickelways of York;
tel: 01904 622303

TRAVEL

Airport
The nearest airport is Leeds Bradford International
Tel: 0113 250 9696

Bus information
National Express buses depart from York Railway Station (map A4).
First York also operates

local services in the area.
Tel: 01904 551400.

Shopmobility
Level 2, Piccadilly
Car Park;
map F5
One of
York's delights is that so many of its streets are pedestrianized, but this can present problems to anyone who finds walking difficult. The answer is Shopmobility, a scheme which provides, free of charge, wheelchairs and powered scooters. Ring for details in advance.
Tel: 01904 679222

Taxis
Ranks at York Railway Station (map A4), Duncombe Place (map D2) and St Saviourgate (map F3–F4).

Train information
York Railway Station is adjacent to Station Road, (map A4).
National Rail Enquiry Service (daily 24 hours):
tel: 08457 484950

PARK AND RIDE

map: see page 100

Although there are city car parks, please note that most traffic is restricted from driving in the city centre during the following times:

11.00–16.00 (Mon–Fri), 10.30–16.30 (Sat) and 12.00–16.00 (Sun).

However, there are four park-and-ride services offering fast and frequent services to the heart of the city. These operate every ten minutes from 7.00 to 20.00 (Mon–Sat). For Sunday services, tel: 01904 551400. Park and rides at:

White Line Askham Bar; A64/A1036 junction

Yellow Line Grimston Bar; A64/A1079 junction

Green Line Rawcliffe Bar; A1237/A19 north junction

Red Line Designer Outlet; A64/A19 junction

BANKS

Barclays, 1–3 Parliament Street; map E4

Halifax, 47 Parliament Street; map E4

HSBC, 13 Parliament Street; map E4

Lloyds TSB, 5 St Helen's Square; map D3

NatWest, 1 Market Street; map E4

Royal Bank of Scotland, 6 Nessgate; map E5

MAIN POST OFFICE

Lendal; map D3

SPORT

Edmund Wilson Swimming Pool, Thanet Road; Tel: 01904 793031

Megabowl, Stirling Road, Unit 12, Clifton Moor Retail Park; Tel: 01904 690006

Oaklands Sports Centre, Cornlands Road; Tel: 01904 782841

Waterworld, Monks Cross; Tel: 01904 642111

Yearsley Swimming Pool, Haleys Terrace; Tel: 01904 622773

EMERGENCIES

Fire, ambulance or police
Tel: 999

York Police Station
Clifford Street; map E5
Tel: 01904 631321

York District Hospital
Wigginton Road (including accident and emergency)
Tel: 01904 631313

NHS Direct
Tel: 0845 4647

Emergency breakdown
Aaron Services,
92a Huntington Road
Tel: 01904 611161

24-hour petrol stations
Tesco in Tadcaster Road, Dringhouses
Tel: 01904 887400
and in Clifton Moor Retail Park
Tel: 01904 880400

INDEX

CITY-BREAK GUIDES

These full-colour guides come with stunning new photography capturing the special essence of some of Britain's loveliest cities. Each is divided into easy-reference sections where you will find something for everyone – from walk maps to fabulous shopping, from sightseeing highlights to keeping the kids entertained, from recommended restaurants to tours and trips … and much, much more.

BATH

Stylish and sophisticated – just two adjectives that sum up the delightful Roman city of Bath, which saw a resurgence of popularity in Georgian times and in the 21st century is once again a vibrant and exciting place to be.

BRIGHTON

Famous for its piers, the magnificent Royal Pavilion, its huge choice of shops and restaurants and nightclubs, candyfloss and fairground rides, its shingly beach and deckchairs, its art, its culture – Brighton's got the lot.

CAMBRIDGE

Historic architecture mingles with hi-tech revolution in the university city of Cambridge, where stunning skylines over surrounding fenland meet the style and sophistication of modern city living.

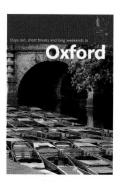

CHESTER

Savour the historic delights of the Roman walls and charming black-and-white architecture, blending seamlessly with the contemporary shopping experience that make Chester such an exhilarating city.

EDINBURGH

Everyone falls in love with Edinburgh, with its Old and New Towns, where a lively café culture, fabulous shops and modern museums sit easily in ancient streets where bloody battles and royal pageant have played their part.

OXFORD

City and university life intertwine in Oxford, with its museums, bookstores and all manner of sophisticated entertainment to entice visitors to its hidden alleyways, splendid quadrangles and skyline of dreaming spires.

STRATFORD

Universally appealing, the picturesque streets of Stratford draw visitors back time and again to explore Shakespeare's birthplace, but also to relish the theatres and stylish riverside town that exists today.

Pitkin Publishing, Healey House, Dene Road, Andover, Hampshire, SP10 2AA, UK
Sales: 01264 409206 Enquiries: 01264 409200 Fax: 01264 334110
e-mail: sales@thehistorypress.co.uk website: www.thehistorypress.co.uk

MAIN ROUTES IN AND OUT OF YORK

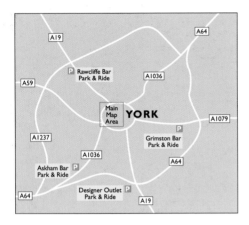

Park and ride services leave regularly for central York from:

Askham Bar Park and Ride
A64/A1036 junction

Grimston Bar Park and Ride
A64/A1079 junction

Rawcliffe Bar Park and Ride
A1237/A19 north junction

Designer Outlet Park and Ride
A64/A19 junction

See page 95 for further details